KT-496-804

THE ESSENTIAL STUDENT COOKBOOK

Cas Clarke wrote her first book, *Grub on a Grant*, after taking a degree in Urban Studies at Sussex University. She now lives in a rural retreat in Surrey with her husband Andy and children James and Helena.

Also by Cas Clarke

Grub on a Grant
Feast Your Friends
Peckish but Poor
Mean Beans
Posh Nosh
Vegetarian Grub on a Grant
Great Grub for Toddlers
More Grub on Less Grant

The Essential Student Cookbook

Cas Clarke

headline

Copyright © 1996, 1999 and 2002 Cas Clarke

The right of Cas Clarke to be identified as the Author of
the Work has been asserted by her in accordance with the
Copyright, Designs and Patents Act 1988.

First published in 2002
by HEADLINE BOOK PUBLISHING

10 9 8 7 6 5 4

Recipes contained within this volume were previously published in
Vegetarian Grub on a Grant and *More Grub on Less Grant*

All rights reserved. No part of this publication may be
reproduced, stored in a retrieval system, or transmitted,
in any form or by any means, without the prior written
permission of the publisher, nor be otherwise circulated
in any form of binding or cover other than that in which
it is published and without a similar condition being
imposed on the subsequent purchaser.

Illustrations by Mik Brown and Mike Gordon

ISBN 0 7553 1056 X

Typeset by
Letterpart Limited, Reigate, Surrey

Printed and bound in Great Britain by
Clays Ltd, St Ives plc

HEADLINE BOOK PUBLISHING
A division of Hodder Headline
338 Euston Road
London NW1 3BH

www.headline.co.uk
www.hodderheadline.com

For my friends and family with all my love

Contents

Foreword

Here are the collected recipes from two of my most successful cookery books. The combined contents from *More Grub on Less Grant* and *Vegetarian Grub on a Grant* are reproduced here under one cover, offering even better value for the next generation of students. On the whole I have left the text as it first appeared, only tinkering with certain aspects. I have updated the symbols in *Vegetarian Grub on a Grant* so that they match its sister book and combined the introductions so that information is not replicated.

I hope that this book will help all those embarking on this exciting part of their life, which hopefully will be instrumental in helping them realise their future dreams.

Introduction

The original *Grub on a Grant* was written in 1984 and was followed up by *More Grub on Less Grant* in 1999. In those intervening years there has been a revolution in the way we shop and eat. Superstores are now commonplace and stock a wealth of exotic produce that has never before been available to us. Most people now are much more aware of what they eat and embrace more cosmopolitan flavours and ideas in cooking. Students have always been keen on big gutsy flavours – this is why dishes such as curry and chilli are enduringly popular – but there is a growing need as the tempo of life continues to increase for methods of cooking which produce meals quickly and easily, hence the popularity of stir-fried dishes, for example.

However, the biggest change of all has been the increasing emphasis on health and the realisation of how big a part our diet plays in keeping us fit. Fruit and vegetables have been made the focal point of our meals to be matched with rice, potatoes, noodles, pasta or bread to meet our energy needs and just a little protein. The protein that we eat now is much more likely to be of vegetable origin; long gone are the days when it was thought that proteins from vegetable sources were second class. Half of this book is for vegetarian dishes but there are also many other recipes from *More Grub on Less Grant* that are suitable both for vegetarians and vegans. The reason for this is, of course, that vegetarian cooking tends to be less expensive than cooking with meat.

When all is said and done, the most important factor in *student* cookery is cost. That doesn't mean that a student can't eat well, it's just a matter of keeping away from costly items such as takeaways and ready made meals. Students also have particular problems (especially in halls of residence) with storage and facilities.

I am confident that this bumper edition will show you how to overcome the problems of catering and that with it as a guide, you too can become a competent cook who enjoys cooking both for yourself and for friends. I still firmly believe that nothing beats an evening spent with friends, wining and dining!

1 Handy Hints

- The measures in all the recipes are approximate, so don't worry if the tin or jar you buy differs slightly from the one that I have used. The only time you need to be more careful is when you are cooking rice or baking. Different types of rice can absorb varying amounts of liquid, so be aware of this and keep an eye on these dishes. If you think the dish is drying out before it is cooked, turn the heat down and/or add a little more liquid.

- Ovens vary enormously. If dishes are coming out overdone, turn the heat down by 10°C/25°F/Gas 1 whenever you cook. Conversely, if dishes always take longer increase the temperature by the same amount.

- Make sure if a recipe says 'gently simmer' that this is what you do, otherwise you could end up with a burnt pan and food. When grilling make sure if cooking fatty meat that you beware of spitting fat or you could end up with a flash fire!

- Quantities of seasonings given are for your guidance only; if you don't like something, omit it or replace it with something else. Alter how much chilli or curry powder you add to suit your own (and your guests') tastes.

- Some recipes use canned beans – to save even more money you can buy them dried, then soak and cook them yourself (if you think the money saved is worth the effort). Use half as many dried beans as the recipe asks for. Soak them overnight, then drain and boil them for 10 minutes (this gets

rid of any toxins in the beans and is essential).
Simmer for 1–1½ hours until the beans are soft.

- If you have half a can of something left over,
  transfer it to a container – a pudding bowl with a
  plate over it will do – and keep it in the fridge. If
  left in the can it may develop a metallic taste.

- It's useful to have a plastic storage box with your
  name on it to keep items in the fridge. It's also
  useful to have some clingfilm to wrap half used-up
  vegetables in – buy the local supermarket's
  economy version.

- Buy your local supermarket's economy version
  whenever possible to make huge savings on baked
  beans, kidney beans, spaghetti, pasta and rice.
  Although I often specify cans of chopped tomatoes
  (being extremely lazy myself), it is cheaper if you
  buy the economy version and chop them yourself.
  Beware of buying a smaller can that is actually
  more expensive than the bigger size! You will save
  money even if you end up wasting half of it.

- Watch out for foodstuffs that have to be kept in the
  fridge. With fewer preservatives in food many more
  items, once opened, have to be stored in the fridge
  and used up within a specified time. You ignore this
  at your peril, as the dangers of food poisoning are
  all too real and each year the number of cases goes
  up.

- In this book, because by nature I am extremely
  lazy, I have used minced chilli and ginger in many
  recipes. Where minced chilli has been used you
  can substitute either ground chilli, dried chilli flakes
  or a fresh chilli, deseeded and finely chopped. Use
  whichever is most convenient for you – minced

chilli wins hands down for me as the work has
been done and the appearance is good when mixed
into a dish. Its drawback is that it has to be kept in
the fridge and used up within six weeks so if this is
a problem for you I would suggest buying either
dried chillis which can be crumbled into your
cooking or buying them fresh as needs dictate.
Minced ginger has the same drawbacks as chilli but
is even more convenient to use. However, you can
substitute fresh ginger, peeled and grated, or very
finely diced. A chunk about 3cm long is roughly
the same amount as a rounded teaspoonful of
minced ginger.

- Symbols used in headings:

V – Suitable for vegetarians
Ve – Suitable for vegans
✳ – Can be cooked using only one ring on the cooker,
or no cooking required
◔ – This recipe can be made in half an hour or less

Items to take to college

Essential

knife
tin opener
wooden spoon
cutlery and crockery
tea-towel
one-person casserole dish

small saucepan
large saucepan with lid
frying pan
baking tray
chopping board

Really useful
colander or sieve
measuring spoons and jug
mixing bowl
whisk
cheese grater
garlic press
20cm flan tin – for pastry dishes and some sweet dishes
corkscrew

For cooking with friends
large casserole dish
lasagne dish
a second large saucepan

Basic store cupboard

coffee
tea
sugar (if used)
milk (if used)   Essential to get you through
margarine/butter   your first night/morning
eggs and/or cheese   before the shops open
bread

The ideal parents would also supply

dried bean mix   balti paste
rice   mango chutney
pasta   tomato purée
cornflour   vegetable stock cubes
split red lentils   mixed herbs
breakfast cereal   oregano
Marmite   salt and pepper
peanut butter   can chick peas
tomato ketchup   can baked beans
soy sauce   can sweetcorn
oil   can chopped tomatoes

And some fresh vegetables to start you off

potatoes   mushrooms
onions   tomatoes
green pepper   carrots
garlic   courgettes

2 The Hairy Hall Experience

What makes cooking conditions so different in halls of residence?

Firstly, facilities are generally not up to much. It is not unknown for 12–20 students to have to share one cooker, so anyone who hogs the cooker is not going to be popular. These recipes are fast and only a couple use the actual oven; most are stir-fried.

Fridge space is also at a premium and the contents of fridges are susceptible to being stolen, so items that have to be refrigerated have been kept to a minimum. Freezers are unknown in most halls – only the ice-box in the fridge is available, so I have used just two products that are bought frozen (and can be bought on campus the day you intend to use them). I have assumed, too, that little money is available for a stock cupboard so such items do not feature heavily.

I know that it can be difficult to buy really fresh vegetables on campus and here I have kept mainly to the veggie staples of the student diet, i.e. onions, peppers, tomatoes, mushrooms and carrots. However, even with all these problems it can still be possible to eat well when in hall. In the recipes in this book I have used items such as minced chilli and ginger because of the convenience factor. Since they have to be kept in the fridge and you may have problems with marauding bands of thieves or 'borrowers', all of these items can be bought fresh in small quantities in supermarkets (and sometimes even from campus shops).

These recipes are quick and easy to make and very cosmopolitan in flavour. There are also a few recipes in Chapter 6 that are very well suited to hall life.

If a group of you are going to pool resources it is generally cheaper to use recipes from Chapter 10 rather than double up the quantities here. If you are getting together for a special Sunday lunch you will find suitable recipes in Chapter 5 and a whole chapter dedicated to vegetarian Sunday lunches in Chapter 11.

Quick Creamy Curry Sauce
Serves 1
✳ ◔ **V**

Ingredients
  1 tablespoon (15ml) oil
  1 onion, chopped
  2 teaspoons curry powder
  1 tablespoon (15ml) mango chutney
  142ml carton double cream

Method
Heat the oil and fry the onion until soft and starting to brown.
Mix together the rest of the ingredients, then add to the pan.
Stir until the sauce thickens slightly. Use to coat cooked
vegetables, beans or hard-boiled eggs.

Tip
Serve with some more mango chutney on the side.

Macaroni Magic
Serves 2
🕐 **V**

Ingredients
  1 tablespoon (15ml) oil
  1 onion, chopped
  125g quick-cook macaroni
  330ml ready-made cheese sauce
  1 teaspoon (5ml) minced chilli or Dijon mustard
  2 tomatoes, sliced
  50g cheese, grated

Method
Heat the oil and fry the onion until brown. Meanwhile, cook the macaroni in boiling water, according to the packet instructions, then drain. Preheat the grill. Mix together the cheese sauce and chilli or mustard and combine with the macaroni. Place in a heatproof dish and cover with the tomatoes and cheese. Grill until the cheese bubbles and browns.

Tip
Serve with a green salad.

Bean Salsa
Serves 2
✳ ⏱ **V Ve**

Ingredients
400g can mixed beans, drained
2 tomatoes, chopped
½ red pepper, deseeded and finely diced
½ bunch of spring onions, sliced
1 teaspoon (5ml) minced chilli
1 tablespoon (15ml) oil
1 teaspoon (5ml) white wine vinegar
salt and black pepper

Method
Mix together all the ingredients and season.

Tip
Serve with salad and baked potatoes or rice.

Jacket Potato filled with Chilli Beans
Serves 1
V Ve

Ingredients
   1 large potato

For the filling
   215g can chilli beans

Method
Preheat the oven to 220°C/425°F/Gas 7. Prick the potato all over and cook in the preheated oven for 1–1½ hours until crispy outside and soft and fluffy inside. Meanwhile, prepare your filling. Heat the beans gently in a small saucepan. Cut a large cross in the top of the potato and squeeze to open out the potato, then top with the chilli beans.

Tip
Jacket potatoes can also be served with baked, barbecued or curried beans.

Mushroom Stroganoff
Serves 2
✳ ⏲ **V**

Ingredients
>   2 tablespoons (30ml) oil
>   1 onion, thinly sliced
>   250g chestnut mushrooms, sliced
>   1 tablespoon (15ml) whole-grain mustard
>   125ml crème fraîche
>   salt and black pepper

Method
Heat the oil and fry the onion until soft and starting to brown. Add the mushrooms and fry for a few minutes until soft and starting to brown. Stir in the mustard and crème fraîche and just heat through. Season and serve.

Jacket Potatoes filled with Garlic Cheese and Mushrooms
Serves 2
V

Ingredients
2 large potatoes

For the filling
1 tablespoon (15ml) oil
100g button mushrooms, sliced
125g soft cheese with garlic
salt and black pepper

Method
Preheat the oven to 220°C/425°F/Gas 7. Prick the potatoes all over and cook in the preheated oven for 1–1½ hours until crispy outside and soft and fluffy inside. Meanwhile, prepare your filling. Heat the oil and fry the mushrooms until soft and starting to brown. Add the cheese and melt down into a sauce, then season. Cut a large cross in the top of each potato and squeeze gently to open out the potato. Top each potato with the filling.

Chinese Omelette Rolls
Serves 2
✳ ☉ **V**

Ingredients
    4 eggs, beaten
    4 tablespoons chopped parsley
    salt and black pepper
    1 tablespoon (15ml) oil
    1 carrot, grated
    1 courgette, grated
    1 tablespoon (15ml) soy sauce
    1 tablespoon (15ml) tomato ketchup

Method
Beat together the eggs and parsley, then season. Heat the oil and add half the egg mixture. Let the omelette set, drawing back the sides to let any uncooked mixture run underneath. It should only take 2–3 minutes to set. Slide off the pan and repeat with the other omelette. Mix together the remaining ingredients and divide between the two omelettes. Roll up each omelette, then cut in half. Serve immediately.

Tip
You can make these into spicy rolls by adding some minced chilli to the omelette mixture.

Dolcelatte-dressed Spaghetti and Leeks
Serves 2
🕐 **V**

Ingredients
175g spaghetti
1 tablespoon (15ml) oil
1 leek, sliced
75g Dolcelatte cheese, diced
100g soft cheese
salt and black pepper

Method
Cook the spaghetti in boiling water according to the packet instructions. Heat the oil and fry the leek until soft and starting to brown. Add the cheeses and stir while they blend into a smooth sauce. Drain the spaghetti. Season and stir the sauce into the spaghetti, then serve immediately.

Tip
You can substitute 4 × 21g Dolcelatte portions from the pick 'n' mix selection.

Creamy Courgettes and Walnuts
Serves 2
✳ ☉ **V**

Ingredients
      2 tablespoons (30ml) oil
      2 courgettes, cut into matchsticks
      1 celery stick, trimmed and cut into matchsticks
      1 onion, chopped
      125g soft cheese with garlic
      50g walnut pieces
      salt and black pepper

Method
Heat the oil and fry the vegetables for a few minutes until soft and starting to brown. Add the cheese and melt down into a sauce. Stir in the walnuts, season and serve.

Tip
Serve as a topping for pasta or baked potatoes.

Red Pepper and Mushroom Kebabs
Serves 1
* **V Ve**

Ingredients
- ½ red pepper, deseeded and cut into large cubes
- 2 large open mushrooms, quartered
- 2 tablespoons (30ml) soy sauce
- 2 tablespoons (30ml) tomato ketchup

Method
Mix together all the ingredients and leave to marinate for 1 hour. Preheat the grill. Thread the pepper and mushroom alternately on to 2 wooden skewers. Grill for 10 minutes, turning once.

Tip
Soak the wooden skewers in water to prevent them burning under the grill.

Tuna-stuffed Jacket Potatoes
Serves 2

Ingredients
>   2 baking potatoes
>   1 tablespoon (15ml) oil
>   1 small onion, chopped
>   1 clove garlic, crushed
>   105g can tuna, drained and broken into chunks
>   50g soft cheese
>   salt and black pepper
>   2 tablespoons grated Cheddar cheese

Method
Preheat the oven to 200°C/400°F/Gas 6. Prick the potatoes and bake in the preheated oven for 1–1½ hours until cooked through. Meanwhile, heat the oil and fry the onion and garlic until soft and starting to brown at the edges. Remove the potatoes from the oven and preheat the grill. Halve the potatoes and spoon out the flesh. Mix the potato with the onion and garlic, tuna and soft cheese. Season. Place the potato skin shells on a baking dish and stuff with the filling, cover with the grated cheese, then grill until the cheese is melting.

Kidney Bean Kedgeree
Serves 2
🕐 **V**

Ingredients
> 2 eggs
> 1 tablespoon (15ml) oil
> 1 onion, chopped
> 2 teaspoons curry powder
> 125g long-grain rice
> 350ml vegetable stock
> 400g can red kidney beans, drained
> 75ml sour cream
> salt and black pepper
> 2 tomatoes, cut into wedges

Method
Hard-boil the eggs, then plunge into cold water to cool. Shell the eggs and cut into wedges. Meanwhile, heat the oil and fry the onion until soft. Stir in the curry powder and rice. Add the stock, bring to the boil, then cover and simmer for 10–15 minutes until the rice has cooked. Stir through the kidney beans and sour cream. Season and serve garnished with the eggs and tomatoes.

Avocado Salad
Serves 1
✳ ⊕ **V Ve**

Ingredients
>   1 avocado, stoned, peeled and sliced
>   1 little gem lettuce, shredded
>   4cm piece of cucumber, sliced
>   2 tablespoons (30ml) tomato ketchup
>   1 tablespoon (15ml) soy sauce
>   1 teaspoon (5ml) minced chilli
>   1 heaped tablespoon (25g) sunflower seeds

Method
Place the avocado, lettuce and cucumber in a serving bowl. Mix together the tomato ketchup, soy sauce and chilli and use this as a dressing for the salad. Sprinkle with the sunflower seeds.

Tip
Use lettuce and cucumber as a filling for sandwiches – Marmite, lettuce and cucumber is a particularly good combination.

Tomato and Herb Omelette
Serves 1
✳ ☉ **V**

Ingredients
    2 teaspoons (10ml) oil
    3 eggs, beaten
    salt and black pepper
    2 tomatoes, roughly chopped
    1 tablespoon chopped herbs

Method
Heat the oil in a frying pan. Season the eggs and add to the pan. Tip the mixture over the bottom of the pan and draw back the sides to let any uncooked mixture run underneath. Cook for 2–3 minutes until the omelette sets. Add the tomato and herbs, fold over the omelette and slide on to your serving plate.

Tip
Fresh herbs suitable for this are basil, parsley, oregano, tarragon or coriander.

Chicken Chow Mein
Serves 2
✳ ⏲

Ingredients
- 1 tablespoon (15ml) oil
- 1 teaspoon (5ml) minced ginger
- 1 clove garlic, crushed
- 312g packet frozen chicken chow mein
- 1 tablespoon (15ml) soy sauce
- ½ bunch of spring onions, chopped

Method
Heat the oil and stir-fry the ginger and garlic for a few seconds before adding the frozen chicken chow mein. Stir-fry for 3–4 minutes before adding the rest of the ingredients. Cook for another 4 minutes before serving.

Tip
Serve with rice.

There is often very little meat to be bought on campus. However, many campus shops have a freezer tucked away which stocks a small range of frozen foods, and this is where you'll find these packets of frozen chicken chow mein.

Chilli Pizza
Serves 1
✳ ◷ **V**

Ingredients
>1 × 150g pizza base
>2 tablespoons (30ml) tomato purée or ketchup
>400g can plum tomatoes, drained and chopped
>50g cheese, grated
>1 teaspoon (5ml) minced chilli

Method
Preheat the oven to 220°C/425°F/Gas 7. Spread the tomato purée or ketchup over the pizza base. Top with the tomatoes and sprinkle with the cheese and chilli. Bake in the pre-heated oven for 10 minutes until the cheese is bubbling and browning.

Tip
You can make Pizza Margherita by following this recipe but omitting the chilli and adding 1 thinly sliced tomato to the topping.

Undercover Beans (curry version)
Serves 1
V

Ingredients
> 1 tablespoon (15ml) oil
> 1 onion, chopped
> 400g can mixed beans
> 330ml curried gravy made with 50g chip shop curry
> gravy granules
> 2 slices bread, buttered and cut into triangles

Method
Preheat the oven to 180°C/350°F/Gas 4. Heat the oil and fry the onion until starting to brown. Mix in the beans and gravy and transfer to a heatproof dish. Cover with the bread triangles, butter side up. Cook in the preheated oven for 25 minutes.

Chinese Prawns
Serves 2

✳ ◔

Ingredients
>   340g packet frozen Chinese prawns
>   1 teaspoon (5ml) minced ginger
>   1 clove garlic, crushed
>   2 teaspoons (10ml) Thai red curry paste
>   1 tablespoon (15ml) soy sauce

Method
Put all the ingredients in a pan and stir-fry for 5–6 minutes.

Tip
Serve with rice or noodles.

Another useful standby using a frozen dish that can be found in most freezers on campus and in small corner shops.

Golden Bean Curry
Serves 1
✳ ⊕ **V**

Ingredients
> 1 tablespoon (15ml) oil
> 1 onion, chopped
> 1 teaspoon paprika
> 400g can black-eyed beans, drained
> 330ml curried gravy made with 50g chip shop curry
> gravy granules

Method
Heat the oil and fry the onion until brown. Add the paprika and beans and stir through. Add the curried gravy and heat through.

Tip
Serve with rice or chapattis.

Garlicky Beans
Serves 1
✳ ⏱ **V**

Ingredients
    1 tablespoon (15ml) oil
    1 onion, chopped
    2 cloves garlic, crushed
    400g can black-eyed beans, drained
    40g soft cheese with garlic

Method
Heat the oil and fry the onion and garlic until soft and starting to brown. Add the beans and cheese. Stir until the cheese melts into a garlicky sauce.

Tip
Serve with baked potatoes, rice or pasta.

Avocado and Salsa Tortillas
Serves 2
✳ ⊙ **V**

Ingredients
1 avocado
4 tortillas
½ bunch of spring onions, chopped
50g cheese, grated
75ml sour cream
2 tablespoons (30ml) hot salsa

Method
Peel and remove the stone from the avocado, slice and divide among the tortillas. Sprinkle each tortilla with spring onions and cheese. Spoon the sour cream and hot salsa over the tortillas. Wrap up each tortilla and serve.

Tip
These can be served as a snack or served with salad as a main course.

Bean and Cheese-filled Tortillas can be made by filling tortillas with drained, canned beans and grated cheese.

Croque Monsieur
Serves 1
✳ ⏱

Ingredients
2 thin white bread slices
1 teaspoon (5ml) Dijon mustard
2 slices Gruyère cheese
25g thinly sliced ham
butter or margarine, to spread

Method
Preheat the grill. Spread one slice of bread with the mustard, top with 1 slice of Gruyère, then pile on the ham. Top with the other Gruyère slice, then the other bread slice. Spread the outside of the sandwich with butter or margarine and grill each side until brown. Cut into two triangles and serve.

Tip
Cheese and ham make a great filling for sandwiches or use to top omelettes or pizzas.

Scrambled Curried Eggs with Chapattis
Serves 1
🕒 **V**

Ingredients
>   knob of butter
>   1 teaspoon curry powder
>   3 eggs, beaten
>   2 tablespoons (30ml) milk
>   salt and black pepper
>   2 chapattis

Method
Melt the butter in a small saucepan and quickly stir-fry the curry powder for about 20 seconds. Mix together the eggs and milk, season and add to the pan. Stir-fry until the eggs have made a soft set. Meanwhile, heat the chapattis under the grill. Divide the mixture between the chapattis and roll up.

Tip
Serve chapattis instead of rice with curries.

Baked Lemon Chicken
Serves 2
✳

Ingredients
> 4 chicken thighs
> 1 tablespoon (15ml) oil
> juice of ½ lemon
> 1 tablespoon (15ml) soy sauce
> 1 teaspoon sugar

Method
Preheat the oven to 190°C/375°F/Gas 5. Put the chicken thighs in a single layer in an ovenproof dish. Spoon over the oil, lemon juice and soy sauce. Sprinkle with the sugar. Cook in the preheated oven for 35 minutes. Serve hot or cold.

Tip
Serve hot with rice or cold with salad.

Zen Walnuts
Serves 1
☀ ⏱ **V Ve**

Ingredients
        1 tablespoon (15ml) oil
        1 onion, chopped
        100g walnut pieces
        2 tablespoons demerara sugar
        1 tablespoon (15ml) soy sauce

Method
Heat the oil and fry the onion until starting to brown. Add the walnuts and sugar and cook until the sugar starts to caramel-ise. Stir in the soy sauce and serve.

Tip
Serve with rice or noodles.

Chilli Vegetables and Noodles
Serves 1
✳ ◔ **V Ve**

Ingredients
  2 tablespoons (30ml) oil
  1 onion, sliced
  1 large carrot, peeled and cut into matchsticks
  100g mushrooms, thickly sliced
  100g green beans
  85g packet dried noodles, vegetable flavour
  1 tablespoon (15ml) minced chilli

Method
Heat the oil and fry the onion for 3–4 minutes, then add the other vegetables and stir-fry for 2 minutes. Break up the noodles, then add them to the pan with 200ml boiling water and the contents of the seasoning sachet. Stir well, cover and simmer for 3 minutes. Stir in the chilli and serve.

Tip
Alter the amount of chilli to suit your own taste.

Toasted Omelette Sandwich
Serves 1
🕐 **V**

Ingredients
>   1 tablespoon (15ml) oil
>   ½ red pepper, deseeded and sliced
>   75g mushrooms, sliced
>   2 eggs, beaten
>   salt and pepper
>   2 slices bread
>   margarine, to spread

Method
Heat the oil and fry the pepper and mushrooms until soft and starting to brown. Season the eggs, add to the pan and cook until the omelette sets. Meanwhile, toast the bread, then spread each slice with margarine. Place the folded omelette on one slice of the toast, then top with the other slice.

Tip
This is great with tomato ketchup.

Pipérade
Serves 2
* ◐ **V**

Ingredients
>   3 tablespoons (45ml) oil
>   2 onions, thinly sliced
>   1 red pepper, thinly sliced
>   1 green pepper, thinly sliced
>   2 cloves garlic, crushed
>   4 eggs, beaten
>   salt and pepper

Method
Heat the oil and fry the vegetables with the garlic for a few minutes until softening and starting to brown at the edges. Season the eggs and add to the pan. Cook over a gentle heat, stirring gently to allow the eggs to set.

Tip
This is great served with a green salad and crusty French bread or ciabatta.

You can make this for one person, halve the ingredients and substitute just 1 red pepper for the mixed peppers.

Risotto with Mushrooms and Walnuts
Serves 2
✳ ◕ **V Ve**

Ingredients
>1 tablespoon (15ml) oil
>1 onion, chopped
>200g mushrooms, sliced
>125g risotto rice
>450ml vegetable stock
>100g walnuts, broken
>salt and black pepper

Method
Heat the oil and fry the onion until soft. Stir in the mushrooms and rice. Add the stock 150ml at a time and allow this to be absorbed before adding more. When all the stock has been absorbed, stir in the walnuts, season and serve.

Tip
Non-vegans can stir in a little butter just before serving.

Sun-dried Tomato Risotto
Serves 1
✳ ☉ **V**

Ingredients
- 1 tablespoon (15ml) oil
- 1 small onion, chopped
- 65g risotto rice
- 250ml vegetable stock
- 25g Parmesan cheese, grated
- 8 sun-dried tomatoes, chopped or sliced
- salt and black pepper

Method
Heat the oil and fry the onion until brown. Add the rice and one-third of the stock. Cook until this stock is absorbed, then add half the remaining stock. When this too is absorbed add the remaining stock. When all the stock has been absorbed, stir in the cheese and tomatoes and season.

Tip
Risotto is even better if you stir in a little butter just before serving.

Egg and Lentil Curry
Serves 2
🕐 **V**

Ingredients

    3 eggs
    1 tablespoon (15ml) oil
    1 onion, chopped
    2 cloves garlic, crushed
    2 tablespoons medium curry powder
    200ml carton creamed coconut
    400g can brown lentils, drained
    1 tablespoon (15ml) Indian chutney

Method

Place the eggs in a saucepan, cover with cold water and bring to the boil. Cook for 10 minutes. Plunge into cold water to cool. Peel off the shells and cut each in half lengthways. Meanwhile, heat the oil and fry the onion and garlic until starting to brown. Add the curry powder and a little creamed coconut and blend into a sauce. Add the rest of the coconut and the lentils. Cook for a few minutes to thicken the sauce. Stir in the chutney and serve the eggs on top of the lentils.

Serve with rice or chapattis.

Thai Crispy Vegetables
Serves 1
✳ ◷ **V Ve**

Ingredients
>   2 teaspoons (10ml) Thai red curry paste
>   1 tablespoon (15ml) soy sauce
>   1 teaspoon (5ml) minced lemongrass
>   400g can mixed Oriental vegetables, drained

Method
Mix together the curry paste, soy sauce and lemongrass. In a frying pan heat the sauce, then add the vegetables and quickly heat through – do not overcook or they will lose their crunchiness.

Tip
Either buy and finely chop a stem of lemongrass or buy a jar of minced lemongrass if you cook Thai food a lot.

Serve with rice or noodles.

Thai Lamb
Serves 2
✳ ☉

Ingredients
- 1 tablespoon (15ml) oil
- 1 onion, chopped
- 2 cloves garlic, crushed
- 2 teaspoons (10ml) minced ginger
- 150g lamb neck fillet, thinly sliced
- 100g mushrooms, sliced
- ½ bunch of spring onions, sliced
- 1 teaspoon (5ml) minced chilli
- 1 tablespoon (15ml) soy sauce
- 1 teaspoon (5ml) runny honey or demerara sugar

Method
Heat the oil and fry the onion, garlic and ginger for 5 minutes. Add the lamb and cook for another 5 minutes. Add the rest of the ingredients and stir-fry for another 2–3 minutes.

Tip
This is really good with rice and more soy sauce for serving.

Chicken and Banana Creole
Serves 2
⏱

Ingredients
    125g long-grain rice
    330ml chicken stock, made with 1 stock cube and
       boiling water
    2 tablespoons (30ml) oil
    1 medium chicken breast, boned and skinned, cut into
       strips
    1 onion, chopped
    1 clove garlic, crushed
    ½ green pepper, thickly sliced
    400g can red kidney beans, drained and rinsed
    1 teaspoon (5ml) minced chilli
    1 banana, thickly sliced

Method
Place the rice in a pan with a tightly fitting lid and cook gently in the stock until all the stock has been absorbed. Meanwhile, heat the oil and fry the chicken, onion, garlic and pepper until soft and starting to brown. Add the beans, cover and cook until soft. Add the remaining ingredients, mix together well and serve.

Tip
Serve with rice.

Quick-fix Chicken Noodles
Serves 2
✳ ☉

Ingredients
  2 tablespoons (30ml) oil
  1 onion, sliced
  1 chicken breast, sliced
  1 green pepper, deseeded and sliced
  100g broccoli florets
  1 teaspoon (5ml) minced ginger (optional)
  100g packet chow mein flavour dried noodles
  1 tablespoon (15ml) soy sauce

Method
Heat the oil and fry the onion for 3 minutes until starting to brown. Add the chicken and stir-fry for another 3 minutes. Add the pepper, broccoli and ginger (if using), then stir-fry for 2 minutes. Break up the noodles and add them to the pan with 250ml boiling water and the contents of the seasoning packet. Stir, cover and cook for 3–4 minutes or until the water is nearly absorbed. Stir in the soy sauce and serve.

Tip
Serve with rice.

3 Food in a Flash

Once you are living together with some friends, things on the food front certainly improve. Not all students who live in self-catering accommodation are in halls; many are in accommodation with a number of bed rooms which share a living space, kitchen and bathroom. On campus these 'flats' can still be prey to thieves, as many students often do not lock the doors on these communal areas, locking only their own bedrooms. I remember having stuff stolen from the living area (it's all too easy to forget and leave things lying around) and you'll find that even if you have student insurance you are not covered as there was no forced entry.

So remember that if you don't nail down your possessions they will probably walk! These shared accommodations, however, do generally have a more homely feel to them and even though you have not picked the people you are sharing with, it is not uncommon for these to be the very people you will strike up your initial friendships with, then perhaps go on to share accommodation with outside campus. Although most people don't cook and eat together every night, it is usually possible to cook together on some nights and a bonus is that it works out cheaper this way. Cooking and eating together is fun and reflects the big part food plays in our society. Nowadays most people eat out in restaurants fairly regularly, not just on special occasions as was once the norm.

While I was wandering around my old university, doing some research for this book, I dropped in at the students' union and picked up a uni handbook. In the intros to the union reps more than half of them mentioned food when asked what would be involved in their ideal evening (the same proportion that mentioned lcohol as featuring in their ideal evening!)

So although students may not be able to eat out as often as they would like to, it is possible to share a meal, a few drinks and convivial company.

Jacket Potatoes filled with Avocado and Bacon
Serves 4

Ingredients
>   4 large potatoes

For the filling
>   4 rashers bacon, grilled until crispy
>   1 avocado, peeled, stoned and cubed
>   salt and black pepper

Method
Preheat the oven to 220°C/425°F/Gas 7. Prick the potatoes all over and cook in the preheated oven for 1–1½ hours until crispy outside and soft and fluffy inside. Meanwhile, prepare your filling. Crumble or dice the bacon, mix with the avocado, and season. Cut a large cross in the top of each potato and squeeze gently to open out the potato, then top with the filling.

Tricolor Spaghetti
Serves 2
✳ ☉ **V**

Ingredients
175g spaghetti
50ml crème fraîche
1 clove garlic, crushed
2 sun-dried tomatoes, sliced
fresh basil, shredded
40g Parmesan or other hard cheese, cut into slivers
salt and black pepper

Method
Cook the spaghetti in boiling water according to the packet instructions. Meanwhile, mix together the rest of the ingredients except the Parmesan, then season. When the spaghetti is cooked, drain well and return to the pan with the mixed ingredients. Warm through and serve topped with the Parmesan.

Tip
Use a potato peeler to cut fine slivers of cheese for this recipe.

Gado Gado Salad
Serves 4
🕐 **V**

Ingredients

For the salad
   4 eggs
   1 iceberg lettuce, finely shredded
   2 carrots, peeled and cut into fine shavings
   ½ cucumber, peeled and cut into matchsticks

For the peanut dressing
   4 tablespoons crunchy peanut butter
   juice of 1 lime
   1 dessertspoon (10ml) honey or sugar
   1 tablespoon (15ml) soy sauce
   ½ teaspoon (2.5ml) minced chilli

Method
Place the eggs in cold water and bring to the boil. Cook for 10 minutes, then plunge into cold water to cool. Shell the eggs and cut each in half lengthways. Place the salad ingredients in a bowl. Put all the peanut dressing ingredients in a pan and heat gently, stirring until they combine. Drizzle the dressing over the salad and serve immediately.

Spaghetti Putanesca
Serves 4
🕐

Ingredients
> 450g spaghetti
> 2 tablespoons (30ml) oil
> 1 onion, chopped
> 2 cloves garlic, crushed
> 1 tablespoon capers
> 220g can chopped tomatoes
> 100g stoned black olives
> 50g can anchovies in oil, drained

Method
Cook the spaghetti in boiling water according to the packet instructions. Heat the oil and fry the onion and garlic for a few minutes until starting to brown. Add the remaining ingredients, cover tightly and simmer for 10 minutes. When the spaghetti is cooked, drain and serve topped with the sauce.

Tip
This is a very gutsy sauce. If the flavours are too strong for you, try cooking it without the anchovies and adding the olives just before serving.

Sausage and Bean Casserole
Serves 4
🕐

Ingredients
>2 tablespoons (30ml) oil
>16 small sausages
>2 cloves garlic, crushed
>400g can chopped tomatoes
>400g can baked beans
>400g can mixed beans, drained
>1/2 teaspoon dried thyme
>200ml chicken or vegetable stock, made with 1 stock
>   cube and boiling water
>black pepper

Method
Heat the oil and fry the sausages until brown all over. Put the sausages and all the remaining ingredients in a large saucepan and season. Bring to the boil, cover tightly and simmer for 20 minutes.

Tip
This is very good served with garlic bread and salad.

Jacket Potatoes filled with Onions and Sausages
Serves 4

Ingredients
    4 large potatoes

For the filling
    1 tablespoon (15ml) oil
    4 sausages
    1 onion, sliced
    2 tablespoons (30ml) whole-grain mustard

Method
Preheat the oven to 220°C/425°F/Gas 7. Prick the potatoes all over and cook in the preheated oven for 1–1½ hours until crispy outside and soft and fluffy inside. Meanwhile, prepare your filling. Heat the oil and fry the sausages for about 20 minutes until browned all over and cooked inside. Remove from the pan and cut each sausage into large chunks. Add the onion to the pan and fry until brown, then return the sausages to the pan and stir in the mustard. Cut a large cross in the top of each potato and squeeze gently to open out the potato, then top with the onions and sausages.

Cabanos Sausage and Pepper Sauce
(for pasta)
Serves 4
✳ ◔

Ingredients
>2 tablespoons (30ml) oil
>1 onion, sliced
>3 peppers of mixed colours, deseeded and sliced
>2 cloves garlic, crushed
>400g can chopped tomatoes
>1 teaspoon dried oregano
>2 cabanos sausages, peeled and cut into chunks
>salt and black pepper

Method
Heat the oil and fry the onion, peppers and garlic until softened. Add the tomatoes, oregano and sausages, season and cook for 5 minutes to thicken the sauce before serving.

Lamb Korma
Serves 4
✳

Ingredients
>1 tablespoon (15ml) oil
>1 large onion, chopped
>2 cloves garlic, crushed
>225g baking potato, peeled and diced
>500g minced lamb
>1 tablespoon korma curry powder
>200ml boiling water
>2 tablespoons (30ml) Indian chutney
>salt and pepper

Method
Heat the oil and fry the onion and garlic for 5 minutes until soft and starting to brown. Add the potato and lamb and stir-fry for 5 minutes until the meat has browned. Add the rest of the ingredients and season. Bring to the boil, cover tightly and simmer for 20 minutes.

Stuffed Pitta Breads
Serves 4
✳ ◷ **V**

Ingredients
    400g can chick peas, drained
    10cm piece cucumber, diced
    1 avocado, stoned, peeled and diced
    4 spring onions, sliced
    Peanut Butter Sauce (page 162)
    6 pitta breads

Method
Mix together the chick peas, cucumber, avocado and spring
onions and dress with the peanut butter sauce. Grill the pitta
breads until they swell, then cut each in half. Stuff each pitta
bread with the chick pea mixture and serve.

Tortilla-topped Mexican Pie
Serves 4

Ingredients
    2 tablespoons (30ml) oil
    1 leek, sliced
    2 cloves garlic, crushed
    2 carrots, diced
    250g minced beef
    1 teaspoon (5ml) minced chilli
    300ml thick beef gravy, made with 30g gravy granules
        and boiling water
    400g can red kidney beans, drained and rinsed
    30g packet tortilla chips
    25g cheese, grated

Method
Preheat the oven to 200°C/400°F/Gas 6. Heat the oil and fry
the leek, garlic and carrots until softened. Add the beef and
chilli and cook for a further 5 minutes to brown the meat.
Add the gravy and beans, mix well and place in an ovenproof dish. Cover with the tortillas and sprinkle with the
cheese. Bake in the preheated oven for 25 minutes.

Cauliflower, Chick Pea and Tomato Curry
Serves 4
* V Ve

Ingredients
1 tablespoon (15ml) oil
1 large onion, chopped
2 cloves garlic, crushed
4 tablespoons (60ml) medium balti curry paste
1 small cauliflower, divided into florets
375ml vegetable stock, made with 1 stock cube and
    boiling water
4 tomatoes, cut into wedges
400g can chick peas, drained
2 tablespoons (30ml) Indian chutney
salt and black pepper

Method
Heat the oil and fry the onion and garlic until starting to
brown. Stir in the curry paste, add the cauliflower and stock
and bring to the boil, then cover tightly and simmer for 15
minutes. Add the tomatoes, chick peas and chutney and
continue to cook, uncovered, for 10 minutes. Season and
serve.

Tip
If finances allow it, chopped coriander can be added to the
finished dish.

Ham, Mushroom and Basil Sauce
(for pasta)
Serves 4

✳ ◔

Ingredients
>   50g butter
>   2 tablespoons (30ml) olive oil
>   250g button or chestnut mushrooms, thinly sliced
>   100g ham, diced
>   4 tablespoons chopped fresh basil
>   salt and black pepper

Method
Heat the butter and oil and fry the mushrooms until soft and starting to brown. Add the ham and basil, season and serve.

Tip
Tagliatelle is very good with this sauce.

Farfalle with Pepperoni and Olives
Serves 4
🕒

Ingredients
> 400g farfalle pasta
> 2 tablespoons (30ml) oil
> 2 onions, chopped
> 2 cloves garlic, crushed
> 1 teaspoon (5ml) minced chilli
> 400g can chopped tomatoes
> 100g pepperoni, roughly chopped
> 50g stoned black olives

Method
Cook the farfalle in plenty of boiling water according to the packet instructions. Meanwhile, heat the oil and fry the onions and garlic until soft and starting to brown. Add the chilli and tomatoes and simmer, uncovered, for 5 minutes. When the pasta is cooked, drain and divide between 4 serving bowls. Stir the pepperoni and olives into the sauce and spoon over the pasta.

Sweetcorn and Mixed Bean Salad
Serves 4
✳ ⏲ **V**

Ingredients

For the salad
  300g can sweetcorn, drained
  400g can butter beans, drained
  300g can broad beans, drained
  3 celery sticks, sliced
  1 bunch of spring onions, sliced

For the dressing
  2 tablespoons (30ml) oil
  1 tablespoon (15ml) lemon juice
  1 clove garlic
  salt and black pepper
  150g carton natural yogurt

Method
Mix together the salad ingredients in a shallow serving dish.
Whisk together the oil, lemon juice and garlic and combine
with the beans. Season, then drizzle with the yogurt.

Bobotie
Serves 4

Ingredients
- 1 tablespoon (15ml) oil
- 1 onion, chopped
- 2 cloves garlic, crushed
- 1 tablespoon (15ml) medium curry paste
- 500g minced beef
- 2 tablespoons (30ml) tomato purée
- 1 tablespoon (15ml) white wine vinegar
- 50g sultanas
- 2 tablespoons (30ml) mango chutney
- 1 slice bread soaked in 3 tablespoons (45ml) milk, mashed
- 1 banana, mashed
- salt and pepper
- 2 eggs, beaten
- 200ml milk

Method
Preheat the oven to 180°C/350°F/Gas 4. Heat the oil and fry the onion and garlic until starting to brown. Add the curry paste and beef and stir-fry until browned. Add the tomato purée, vinegar, sultanas, chutney, mashed bread and banana. Season and transfer to an ovenproof dish. Mix together the eggs and milk, season and pour over the meat mixture. Bake in the preheated oven for 40 minutes or until the egg mixture has set.

Vegetable Bake
Serves 4
V Ve

Ingredients
>1 aubergine
>3 tablespoons (45ml) olive oil
>4 onions, sliced
>2 cloves garlic, crushed
>200g mushrooms, sliced
>sprinkling of dried thyme
>salt and pepper
>8 tomatoes
>2 courgettes

Method
Preheat the oven to 180°C/350°F/Gas 4. Prick the aubergine all over with a fork and place in a roasting tin. Bake in the preheated oven for 25 minutes, then leave to cool. Meanwhile, heat 2 tablespoons (30ml) of the oil and fry the onions and garlic for 5–10 minutes until softened and starting to brown. Add the mushrooms and stir-fry for a further 2 minutes until starting to soften. Place the onion and mushroom mixture in an ovenproof dish. Skin the aubergine and cube the soft flesh, then stir into the dish. Sprinkle with thyme and season. Slice the tomatoes and courgettes to provide enough slices to arrange them alternately on top of the onion mixture. Season again, drizzle with the remaining oil and bake in the preheated oven for 30–40 minutes until cooked through and the courgettes and tomatoes are starting to brown at the edges.

Tip
As well as being a good vegetarian or vegan main dish this can also be used as a vegetable dish when serving meat, and makes a good addition to a party buffet.

Pasta Pie
Serves 4–6
V

Ingredients
>1 tablespoon (15ml) oil
>450g leeks, sliced
>1 clove garlic, crushed
>4 eggs, beaten
>142ml carton single cream
>125g Gruyère cheese, grated
>125g cooked pasta, roughly chopped
>salt and black pepper

Method
Preheat the oven to 180°C/350°F/Gas 4. Heat the oil and fry the leeks and garlic until soft and starting to brown. Mix the leeks and garlic with all the remaining ingredients, season and place in a greased ovenproof dish or tin. Bake in the preheated oven for 25–30 minutes until the eggs have set and the top is a golden brown colour. Serve hot or cold in wedges.

Rice Medley
Serves 4
✳ ◷

Ingredients
>   2 tablespoons (30ml) oil
>   1 onion, chopped
>   1 red pepper, deseeded and diced
>   1 clove garlic, crushed
>   250g long-grain rice
>   700ml chicken stock
>   salt and black pepper
>   300g can sweetcorn, drained
>   1 bunch of spring onions, chopped
>   185g can tuna in spring water, drained

Method
Heat the oil and fry the onion, pepper and garlic until soft and starting to brown. Stir in the rice, then add the stock. Season and cook, stirring occasionally, until the rice is cooked and has absorbed the stock – about 10–15 minutes. Stir in the rest of the ingredients and serve.

Tip
We like this served with either a sweet chilli sauce or smoky barbecue sauce.

Lamb Kebabs
Serves 4
✳ ◷

Ingredients
> 500g minced lamb
> 2 teaspoons curry powder
> salt and pepper

Method
Preheat the grill. Mix together the lamb and curry powder, then season. Shape into little sausages and thread on to wooden skewers. Cook under the preheated grill for 10 minutes, turning once.

Tip
1 tablespoon chopped mint can be mixed into the kebab mixture. This adds to the flavour, but it's not worth buying mint specifically for this dish.

Bean and Yogurt Salad
Serves 4
✳ ◔ **V**

Ingredients
   2 tablespoons (30ml) oil
   1 onion, chopped
   1 clove garlic, crushed
   1 red pepper, deseeded and cubed
   1 yellow pepper, deseeded and cubed
   2 courgettes, sliced
   4 tomatoes, cut into wedges
   400g can flageolet beans, drained and rinsed
   1 heaped tablespoon raisins
   150g carton natural yogurt

Method
Heat the oil and fry the onion and garlic for a few minutes until starting to soften. Add the peppers and courgettes and cook for a further 5 minutes. Add the tomatoes, beans and raisins, and cook gently just to get the tomato juices running. Allow to cool, then top with the yogurt and serve.

Tip
You can also make this substituting sour cream for the natural yogurt.

Mushroom-stuffed Filo Pie
Serves 4
V Ve

Ingredients
> 2 tablespoons (30ml) oil
> 1 onion, chopped
> 2 cloves garlic, crushed
> 250g chestnut mushrooms, sliced
> 250g button mushrooms, halved
> 1 tablespoon (15ml) soy sauce
> 300ml gravy made with 30g vegetarian gravy granules
> black pepper
> 4 sheets filo pastry
> melted butter

Method
Preheat the oven to 180°C/350°F/Gas 4. Heat the oil and fry the onion and garlic until starting to brown, then add both types of mushroom and stir-fry until soft. Stir in the soy sauce and gravy, season and transfer to an ovenproof dish. Cover with the sheets of filo, brushing each one with melted butter. Arrange them so they overlap, crumpling each sheet at the edges and tucking into the dish. Brush the finished dish with butter and bake in the preheated oven for 15–20 minutes until golden brown.

Tip
Freeze the rest of the pastry for another pie or use to make Feta-filled Filo (page 74).

Chilli, Tomato and Spinach Sauce
(for pasta)
Serves 4
☀ ☉ **V Ve**

Ingredients
- 12 sun-dried tomatoes, and 2 tablespoons (30ml) of the oil from the jar
- 2 cloves garlic, crushed
- 1 teaspoon (5ml) minced chilli
- 690g jar passata (sieved tomatoes)
- 225g fresh baby spinach

Method
Roughly chop the sun-dried tomatoes and fry in the oil with the garlic and chilli for 1 minute. Add the passata and simmer for 5 minutes. Add the spinach and cook until wilted. Serve poured over your favourite pasta.

Cheese and Nut Risotto
Serves 4
✳ ☉ **V**

Ingredients
> 2 tablespoons (60ml) oil
> 1 large onion, chopped
> 2 cloves garlic, crushed
> 250g risotto rice
> 1 teaspoon thyme
> 900ml vegetable stock, made with 2 stock cubes and
>   boiling water
> 100g Parmesan cheese, finely grated
> 100g walnut pieces
> salt and black pepper

Method
Heat the oil and fry the onion and garlic until soft and starting to brown. Add the rice and stir through to coat with oil. Add the thyme and one-third of the stock. Cook until that stock is absorbed, then add half the remaining stock. When that is absorbed add the last of the stock. When all the stock has been absorbed, stir in the Parmesan and walnuts, season and serve.

Hasta Arriba Salad
Serves 4
✳ ◔

Ingredients
    1 tablespoon (15ml) oil
    500g minced beef
    2 cloves garlic, crushed
    1 tablespoon (15ml) tomato purée
    2 teaspoons (10ml) minced chilli
    400g can red kidney beans, drained and rinsed
    2 tablespoons (30ml) salsa
    salt and black pepper

For the salad
    lettuce leaves, shredded
    ½ cucumber, halved lengthways and sliced
    2 tomatoes, cut into wedges
    35g packet tortilla chips

Method
Heat the oil and fry the beef and garlic for 5 minutes until the meat has browned. Stir in the tomato purée. Add the chilli, kidney beans and salsa, season and stir-fry for a few minutes to heat through. Meanwhile, mix together the salad ingredients and divide between 4 bowls. Mix the hot mince into the salad and serve.

Tip
This is great served with crusty bread and some grated cheese and sour cream.

Spaghethai Bolognese
Serves 4
🕐

Ingredients
>   75–100g spaghetti per person
>   1 tablespoon (15ml) oil
>   500g minced pork
>   1 teaspoon (5ml) minced ginger
>   1 teaspoon (5ml) minced lemongrass
>   2 cloves garlic, crushed
>   1 tablespoon (15ml) Thai red curry paste
>   1 tablespoon (15ml) tomato purée
>   1 tablespoon (15ml) soy sauce
>   2 tablespoons chopped spring onions
>   a few basil leaves, roughly torn (optional)

Method
Cook the spaghetti in plenty of boiling water according to the packet instructions. Heat the oil and fry the pork for 5 minutes, stirring to break up any lumps. Add all the remaining ingredients except the spring onions and basil. Stir well and cook for another 5 minutes. Add the spring onions and 200ml water. Simmer for 5 minutes. When the spaghetti is cooked, drain and place in serving bowls. Stir the basil into the sauce and spoon over the spaghetti. Serve.

Tip
This is a very versatile recipe which could even stretch to 6 servings if you served it with more spaghetti. Either finely chop a stem of lemongrass for this recipe or buy some minced lemongrass if you cook a lot of Thai food.

Risi e Bisi
Serves 4
✳ ⏱

Ingredients
>1 tablespoon (15ml) olive oil
>1 tablespoon (15ml) butter
>1 onion, chopped
>2 cloves garlic, crushed
>250g risotto rice
>900ml chicken stock, made with 1 stock cube and
>   boiling water
>450g peas
>25g Parmesan cheese, grated
>100g ham, finely chopped
>1 bunch of parsley, finely chopped
>salt and black pepper

Method
Heat the oil and butter and fry the onion and garlic until starting to brown. Add the rice, give a quick stir, then add 300ml of the stock. Cook until that stock is absorbed, then add another 300ml stock. When that is absorbed add the rest of the stock and the peas. When the stock is nearly absorbed the rice should be cooked. Stir in the Parmesan, ham and parsley, season and serve immediately.

Tuna and Roasted Vegetable Salad
Serves 4
✳

Ingredients
1 aubergine, cut into chunks
2 red peppers, deseeded and sliced
2 red onions, peeled and quartered
1 clove garlic, crushed
4 tablespoons (60ml) olive oil
pinch of oregano
salt and black pepper
185g can tuna, drained and flaked
100g stoned black olives

Method
Preheat the oven to 220°C/425°F/Gas 7. Mix the aubergine, peppers, onions and garlic with the oil and oregano and season. Place on a baking tray and roast in the preheated oven for 30–35 minutes until the vegetables are starting to blacken at the edges. Leave to cool, then serve the vegetables topped with the tuna and olives.

Feta-filled Filo
Serves 4
✳ ◔ **V**

Ingredients
    12 sheets filo pastry
    melted butter

For the filling
    200g feta cheese, crumbled
    100g Gruyère cheese, grated
    2 eggs, beaten
    salt and pepper

Method
Preheat the oven to 180°C/350°F/Gas 4. Mix together the
filling ingredients. Brush a filo sheet with melted butter. Place
some filling in the middle and bottom of the sheet of pastry,
fold each side inwards, then roll the sheet up. (It should look
like a Chinese spring roll.) Brush with more butter and put on
a baking tray. Repeat with the other filo sheets. Bake in the
preheated oven for 15 minutes until light brown in colour.
Serve hot or cold.

Tip
These are great served with garlic bread and salad.

Pork Chilli
Serves 4
✳

Ingredients
    1 tablespoon (15ml) oil
    1 large onion, chopped
    2 cloves garlic, crushed
    1 green pepper, deseeded and diced
    450g minced pork
    1 tablespoon (15ml) minced chilli
    1 teaspoon oregano
    500g carton passata (sieved tomatoes)
    400g can red kidney beans, drained and rinsed

Method
Heat the oil and fry the onion, garlic and pepper for 5–10 minutes until soft and starting to brown. Add the pork and stir-fry for another 5 minutes to brown the meat. Add the rest of the ingredients, bring to the boil, cover and simmer for 20 minutes.

Tip
This can be served with rice, pasta or baked potatoes.

Greek Feta and Vegetable Casserole
Serves 4
🕐 **V**

Ingredients
> 4 tablespoons (60ml) olive oil
> 1 large onion, thinly sliced into rings
> 3 peppers of mixed colours, deseeded and cut into rings
> 4 cloves garlic, crushed
> 4 tomatoes, chopped
> 200g feta cheese, cubed
> 1 teaspoon oregano
> black pepper

Method
Preheat the oven to 200°C/400°F/Gas 6. Heat 3 tablespoons (45ml) of the oil and fry the onion, peppers and garlic until soft and starting to brown. Add the tomatoes and cook for a few more minutes to soften. Transfer to an ovenproof dish and mix in the feta and oregano. Season, drizzle with the remaining oil, cover tightly, then bake in the preheated oven for 15 minutes.

Tandoori Chicken
Serves 4
❋

Ingredients
    8 chicken drumsticks
    8 chicken thighs
    1 tablespoon tikka spice powder
    2 cloves garlic, crushed
    1 tablespoon (15ml) tomato purée
    1 tablespoon (15ml) lemon juice
    75ml sour cream
    salt and pepper

Method
Preheat the oven to its highest temperature. Make deep slashes all over the chicken pieces. Mix together all the rest of the ingredients in a bowl, then add the chicken and cover with the mixture. If you have time, cover and leave in the fridge for a while to marinate, or transfer to an ovenproof dish and cook in the preheated oven for 35 minutes until well cooked and blackening.

Tip
These are lovely served with lemon wedges, tomato and onion slices and a crisp green salad. Cucumber Raita (page 263) also goes well with them.

Green Curry
Serves 2
✳ ◷ **V**

Ingredients
    2 tablespoons (30ml) oil
    1 onion, chopped
    ½ green pepper, deseeded and cubed
    2 cloves garlic, crushed
    1 teaspoon (5ml) minced ginger
    100g green beans, halved
    100g broccoli, divided into small florets
    100g peas
    1 tablespoon medium curry powder
    1 tablespoon (15ml) water
    142ml carton double cream
    15g pack coriander, chopped

Method
Heat the oil and fry the onion, pepper, garlic and ginger until soft and starting to brown. Add the rest of the vegetables and stir-fry for 5 minutes. Whisk together all the remaining ingredients and add to the curry. Heat gently until the sauce thickens slightly.

Tip
This is a good recipe for using up bits and pieces of leftover vegetables.

Dhal and Spinach Curry
Serves 2
✳ ⏱ **V Ve**

Ingredients
- 1 tablespoon (15ml) oil
- 1 onion, chopped
- 1 clove garlic, crushed
- 1 teaspoon (5ml) minced ginger
- 1 teaspoon (5ml) minced chilli
- 2 tablespoons (30ml) medium balti curry paste
- 220g can chopped tomatoes
- 225g fresh or frozen spinach
- 400g can lentil dhal

Method
Heat the oil and fry the onion and garlic until starting to brown. Stir in the rest of the ingredients. When the spinach has wilted into the curry and the curry is hot, serve.

Lebanese Bake
Serves 2

Ingredients
>   250g baby aubergines
>   1 tablespoon (15ml) olive oil
>   1 onion, finely diced
>   250g minced beef
>   ½ teaspoon each of minced ginger, cinnamon and cumin
>   1 tablespoon curry powder
>   125ml water
>   1 tablespoon raisins
>   3 tomatoes
>   few leaves of mint, chopped (optional)

Method
Preheat the oven to 200°C/400°F/Gas 6. Cut the stalk end off each baby aubergine and lay them, cut side upwards, in an ovenproof dish or roasting tin. Heat the oil and fry the onion for a few minutes until starting to brown. Add the beef and stir-fry quickly, breaking up any lumps. Add the spices, curry powder, water and raisins, stir well and cook for a few minutes. Spoon the meat sauce over the baby aubergines, then cut the tomatoes into thick slices (about 3 or 4 from each tomato) and surround the aubergines with these. Sprinkle with the mint (if using). Cover the dish with roasting foil or a tight-fitting lid and cook for 50–60 minutes, until the aubergine is well cooked and soft.

Tip
Serve with rice or pitta bread and Cucumber Raita (page 263). If you can't get baby aubergines (usually from Asian grocers) use 2 larger aubergines and, after halving them, prick them all over to help them cook through.

For a veggie version of this dish substitute 200g finely chopped mushrooms for the minced meat and add some more oil when frying.

Parsley Pesto
Serves 1
✳ ◷ **V**

Ingredients
>   15g pack parsley, chopped
>   2 tablespoons Parmesan cheese, finely grated
>   2 tablespoons finely chopped walnuts
>   2 teaspoons (10ml) oil

Method
Mix together all the ingredients. Serve as a topping for your favourite pasta.

Tip
You can substitute finely chopped pine nuts for the walnuts.

Greek-style Salad
Serves 4
✳ ⏲ **V**

Ingredients
    4 tomatoes, cut into wedges
    ½ cucumber, halved lengthways and sliced
    1 green pepper, deseeded and cut into rings or thinly
       sliced
    1 onion, thinly sliced into rings
    200g feta cheese, cubed
    100g black stoned olives
    salt and black pepper
    4 tablespoons (60ml) olive oil
    1 bunch of parsley, chopped

Method
Arrange the salad vegetables in your serving dish/es. Top
with the feta and olives. Season and drizzle over the oil.
Sprinkle with the parsley and serve.

Tip
The parsley is an integral part of this dish, not just a garnish.

Chicken and Mango Pilau
Serves 2

🕒

Ingredients
> 250g basmati rice
> 2 tablespoons (30ml) oil
> 2 leeks, sliced
> 2 medium chicken breasts, thinly sliced
> 150ml chicken stock, made with 1 stock cube and
>   boiling water
> 4 tablespoons (60ml) mango chutney
> black pepper

Method
Cook the rice in boiling water until tender (approximately 10 minutes). Meanwhile, heat the oil and stir-fry the leeks and chicken until cooked and brown. When the rice is cooked, drain well and combine with the leeks and chicken. Add the stock and chutney, mix well and cook for a few minutes until the stock is incorporated into the dish. Season and serve.

Tip
This is good served with a green salad.

Quick Curry for One
Serves 1
✳ ◷

Ingredients
      1 tablespoon (15ml) oil
      1 small onion, chopped
      ½ red pepper, deseeded and diced
      1 clove garlic, crushed
      125g minced beef
      2 teaspoons medium curry powder
      75g basmati rice
      200ml boiling water
      1 tablespoon (15ml) Indian chutney

Method
Heat the oil and fry the onion, pepper and garlic for 5 minutes until soft and starting to brown. Add the beef and stir-fry for another 5 minutes until browned. Add the rest of the ingredients and bring to the boil. Cover tightly and simmer for 10 minutes. Remove from the heat and leave to stand for 5 minutes before serving.

Tip
For an even more impressive curry add ½ teaspoon whole cumin or coriander seeds just before you add the rest of the ingredients.

Mozzarella-topped Spinach and Potato Gratin
Serves 4
V

Ingredients
> 600g potatoes, peeled and thinly sliced
> 500g fresh spinach, cleaned and washed
> 200g mozzarella cheese, grated
> salt and black pepper
> 4 tomatoes, sliced
> 3 eggs, beaten
> 284ml carton whipping cream

Method
Preheat the oven to 180°C/350°F/Gas 4. Cook the potatoes in boiling water for 5 minutes, then drain well. Meanwhile, cook the spinach in boiling water for 5 minutes, drain and squeeze out excess water. Grease a large casserole dish and line the bottom with half the potatoes, cover with the spinach and half the cheese, seasoning each layer well. Cover with the rest of the potatoes and arrange the tomato slices on top. Sprinkle with the remaining cheese. Whisk together the eggs and cream, season and pour over the dish. Bake in the preheated oven for 55 minutes.

Tip
It is worth getting a friend to help with the preparation of this dish. You can buy bags of grated mozzarella but this is more expensive.

Italian Fish Bake
Serves 4

Ingredients
> 450g cod fillets
> 1 dessertspoon (10ml) lemon juice
> 15g butter
> 1 large onion, chopped
> 2 cloves garlic, crushed
> 400g can chopped tomatoes
> 50g stoned black olives
> black pepper
> 100g mozzarella cheese, grated or thinly sliced

Method
Preheat the oven to 200°C/400°F/Gas 6. Cut the fish into equal size portions and put in a greased ovenproof dish. Squeeze over the lemon juice. Heat the butter and fry the onion and garlic until soft and starting to brown. Add the tomatoes and olives to the pan, stir well, season, then use to cover the fish. Top with the cheese and bake in the preheated oven for 30 minutes until the cheese is golden.

Tip
If you have any capers add some to this dish before including the cheese.

Thai Peanutty Pork
Serves 2

✳ ☉

Ingredients
   1 tablespoon (15ml) oil
   1 onion, chopped
   1 red pepper, chopped
   2 cloves garlic, crushed
   250g minced pork
   1 tablespoon (15ml) Thai red curry paste
   1 tablespoon (15ml) crunchy peanut butter
   1 tablespoon (15ml) soy sauce
   100ml water
   handful of basil, shredded (optional)
   handful of coriander (optional)

Method
Heat the oil and fry the onion and pepper for 5 minutes. Add the garlic and pork and fry for a further 5 minutes. Add the rest of the ingredients except the herbs and stir-fry for 2 minutes. Stir in the herbs (if using) just before serving.

Tip
This dish goes really well with noodles but can be served with rice if you prefer.

Sri Lankan Curry
Serves 4
✳ ☉

Ingredients
    1 tablespoon (15ml) oil
    1 large onion, chopped
    2 cloves garlic, crushed
    8 chicken thighs, skinned and boned, cut into cubes
    2 tablespoons (30ml) medium balti curry paste
    1 teaspoon (5ml) minced chilli
    1 teaspoon cinnamon
    200ml carton coconut cream

Method
Heat the oil and fry the onion and garlic until soft and browned. Add the chicken and fry for another 5 minutes. Add the curry paste, chilli and cinnamon and stir-fry for 1 minute. Add the coconut cream, stir, cover and simmer for 5–10 minutes, until the chicken is cooked through.

Thai Prawn Curry
Serves 4

✳ ◔

Ingredients
- 1 tablespoon (15ml) oil
- 1 onion, chopped
- 1 clove garlic, crushed
- 1 teaspoon (5ml) minced ginger
- 1 tablespoon (15ml) Thai red curry paste
- 400g can coconut milk
- 450g frozen large, uncooked prawns, defrosted
- fresh coriander leaves, shredded

Method
Heat the oil and fry the onion, garlic and ginger until the onion is softened and starting to brown. Blend in the curry paste with a little of the coconut milk, then add the rest of the coconut milk. Cook, uncovered, until the sauce has reduced and thickened a little. Add the prawns and cook for a few minutes until they have cooked through (they change colour). Stir in the coriander leaves and serve immediately.

Chip-topped Shepherd's Pie
Serves 2–3

Ingredients
1 tablespoon (15ml) oil
1 onion, chopped
1 carrot, diced
500g minced beef
2 teaspoons (10ml) Worcestershire sauce (optional)
375ml gravy, made with 60g gravy granules and
    boiling water
salt and black pepper
500g potatoes, peeled and cut into small thin chips

Method
Preheat the oven to 180°C/350°F/Gas 4. Heat the oil and fry the onion and carrot for about 10 minutes until soft and starting to brown. Add the beef and stir-fry until browned. Combine the Worcestershire sauce (if using) and gravy and stir into the mince. Season. Transfer to an ovenproof dish and cover with the chipped potatoes. Cover tightly and cook in the preheated oven for 30 minutes. Uncover, increase the temperature to 200°C/400°F/Gas 6 and cook for another 20 minutes to brown the chips.

Teriyaki Chicken Stir-fry
Serves 4
⏱

Ingredients
- 2 medium boneless, skinless chicken breasts, cut into thin strips
- 2 tablespoons (30ml) soy sauce
- 1 tablespoon (15ml) oil
- 2 large carrots, peeled and cut into small matchsticks
- 1 red pepper, deseeded and cut into small matchsticks
- 1 green pepper, deseeded and cut into small matchsticks
- 150g jar Sharwood's Teriyaki stir-fry sauce
- 1 bunch of spring onions, chopped

Method
Marinate the chicken in the soy sauce for 20 minutes. Heat the oil in a frying pan and fry the chicken and marinade for 2 minutes. Add the carrots and both peppers and stir-fry for 4 minutes. Add the sauce and spring onions and warm through. Serve.

4 Cooking for a Crowd

Occasionally it is nice to get together with a group of friends for a really good meal and a few drinks. This might be for a specific reason or just because the sun is shining and it feels like a good idea.

Over many years I have come to the conclusion that the easiest way of entertaining large numbers is to have most of the dishes already prepared, so I rely increasingly on salads that can be made up and will sit happily for a time while other last-minute preparations are in hand. For these salads I have drawn on inspiration from many different cultures. I used to theme meals, but nowadays just mix and match as I feel like it. Luckily this coincides with the growth of 'Pacific rim' style cookery, in which West meets East, taking the best from each culture and mixing and matching to provide new and interesting menus.

These recipes cater for 8 or more.

When catering for vegetarians you can produce a feast by serving a selection of the different salads. I would serve 2 vegetarian salads as a substitute for a main course containing meat. Don't forget that even when feeding meat-eaters the main dish can also be a salad. Those containing tuna fish are great substitutes for a hot main dish.

Some points to bear in mind:

Catering for up to 8
Serve 1 starter, 2 salads and 1 main dish.

Catering for 9–12
Serve 2 starters, 3 salads and the Jambalaya (page 114).

Catering for 13–16
Serve 2 starters, 4 salads and 2 main courses.

Serve some French sticks or garlic bread alongside these dishes. As a treat you could provide a pudding. There are many to choose from in the shops, or you could make the very simple Eton Mess which is a mixture of whipped cream, strawberries and broken meringues. You will find the recipe on page 184.

Some people like to get together and decide on a sum which will cover drink as well, or just share the cost of the cooking and get everyone to bring their own favourite drink (which works well if you have a mixture of heavy drinkers and teetotallers).

Some example menus would be:

Least expensive menu for 12
Chilli Olives (page 96)
Tapenade-topped Croûtes (page 97)
Potatoes in Red Pesto (page 102)
Yogurt-dressed Mushroom Salad (page 100)
Algerian Tomato and Pepper Salad (page 101)
Jambalaya (page 114)
6 French sticks

Most expensive menu for 8
Bruschetta (page 99)
Mushrooms à la Grecque (page 108)
Roasted Pepper Salad (page 109)
Mediterranean Lemon Chicken with Olives (page 116)
4 French sticks

Vegetarian meal for 12
Chilli Olives (page 96)
Caponata (page 98) and tortilla chips
Potatoes in Red Pesto (page 102)
Garlic Mushroom Salad (page 103)
Carrot, Egg and Olive Salad (page 104)
Couscous with Fruit and Nuts (page 106)
Roasted Pepper Salad (page 109)
5 French sticks

Starters

Chilli Olives
Serves 8
✳ ◷ **V Ve**

Ingredients
>200g jar green olives with lemon and mint, drained
>2 teaspoons (10ml) minced chilli

Method
Mix together the ingredients and put in a serving bowl.

Tapenade-topped Croûtes
Makes 20–30
✳ ☉ **V Ve**

Ingredients
    7 tablespoons (100ml) olive oil
    4 cloves garlic, crushed
    1 French stick, sliced
    90g jar sun-dried tomato tapenade

Method
Preheat the oven to 180°C/350°F/Gas 4. Mix together the oil and garlic and coat each bread slice with this. Lay the bread on baking sheets and bake in the preheated oven for 15–20 minutes until brown and crisp. Serve each croûte with a little tapenade spread on top.

Tip
Watch these carefully when you bake them as they burn very easily.

Caponata
Serves 8
* **V Ve**

Ingredients
2 aubergines, diced
1 onion, chopped
4 tablespoons (60ml) oil
4 large beef tomatoes, chopped
2 celery sticks, chopped
75g stoned green olives, chopped
2 tablespoons capers, drained and rinsed
4 tablespoons (60ml) white wine vinegar
1 tablespoon sugar

Method
Preheat the oven to 200°C/400°F/Gas 6. Mix together the aubergines, onion and oil and spread out on a baking tray. Cook in the preheated oven for 10 minutes, then add the tomatoes and cook for a further 10 minutes. Remove from the oven and put into a serving dish with the rest of the ingredients (use the juices as well). Stir well and leave to cool before serving.

Bruschetta
Serves 8
🕐 **V**

Ingredients
> 1 ciabatta loaf, cut into 16 slices, toasted
> 2 tablespoons (30ml) olive oil
> 4 tomatoes, sliced
> 200g mozzarella cheese, drained and thinly sliced
> 1 teaspoon oregano
> black pepper
> 100g stoned black olives

Method
Preheat the oven to 220°C/425°F/Gas 7. Place the slices of toast in one layer on a baking tray. Drizzle with 1 tablespoon (15ml) of the oil. Cover with the tomatoes, then the mozzarella, sprinkle with the oregano and season. Bake in the preheated oven for 10 minutes until the cheese has melted. Dribble the remaining oil over the toast and garnish with the olives before serving hot.

Tip
You will need bread to mop up the juices as this is a very messy starter, but absolutely delicious!

Salads

Yogurt-dressed Mushroom Salad
Serves 8
* **V**

Ingredients
  500g chestnut mushrooms, sliced
  150g carton natural yogurt
  juice of ½ lemon
  salt and black pepper

Method
Mix together the mushrooms, yogurt and lemon juice. Do
not season yet. Leave to marinate for 1 hour. Season just
before serving.

Algerian Tomato and Pepper Salad
Serves 8
✳ ◔ **V Ve**

Ingredients
>   3 tablespoons (45ml) olive oil
>   4 peppers of mixed colours, deseeded and sliced
>   8 tomatoes, cut into wedges
>   4 cloves garlic, crushed
>   2 teaspoons (10ml) minced chilli

Method
Heat the oil and fry the peppers until soft and starting to brown. Add the rest of the ingredients and stir-fry until the tomatoes are just beginning to soften. Place in a serving dish and leave to cool.

Potatoes in Red Pesto
Serves 8
✳ ◔ **V**

Ingredients
>1kg baby new potatoes, cooked and cooled
>170g jar or carton fresh red pesto

Method
Mix together the potatoes and pesto and serve.

Garlic Mushroom Salad
Serves 8
✳ ◷ **V**

Ingredients
> 4 tablespoons (60ml) olive oil
> 500g button mushrooms
> 6 cloves garlic, crushed
> 142ml carton sour cream with chives and onions
> salt and black pepper

Method
Heat the oil and fry the mushrooms and garlic for a few minutes – just enough to soften them. Leave to cool, then combine with the sour cream. Season and serve.

Carrot, Egg and Olive Salad
Serves 8
🕐 **V**

Ingredients
    4 eggs
    800g carrots, grated
    juice of ½ lemon
    2 tablespoons black mustard seeds
    3 tablespoons (45ml) oil
    200g mixed olives, drained
    salt and black pepper

Method
Put the eggs in a saucepan, cover with cold water and bring
to the boil. Simmer for 10 minutes. Plunge into cold water to
cool. Peel off the shells and cut each in half lengthways.
Meanwhile, mix together the carrots, lemon juice and mustard seeds. Heat the oil in a frying pan, add the carrot
mixture and stir-fry until the carrot is just softening and the
seeds begin to pop, then remove immediately. Put the
contents of the pan in the middle of a serving dish and
surround with the egg halves and olives. Season and serve.

Tip
Half the prep time of this dish is taken up by grating the
carrots, so if you can get some help here you can save time.

Use the black mustard seeds to give a tang to other salads or
use up when cooking curries.

Tomato and Mozzarella Salad
Serves 8
🕐 **V**

Ingredients
8 tomatoes, sliced
400g mozzarella cheese, sliced
4 tablespoons (60ml) olive oil
2 tablespoons (30ml) white wine vinegar
pinch of sugar
salt and black pepper

Method
Arrange alternate slices of tomato and cheese on each plate.
Put the rest of the ingredients in a screw-top jar and shake
well. Drizzle the dressing all over the salad.

Tip
This is a dish where the better the oil used, the better the
finished dish.

If you are serving with other dishes which use basil, keep a
few sprigs back to garnish this salad.

Couscous with Fruit and Nuts
Serves 8
✳ ☉ **V Ve**

Ingredients
>   250g couscous
>   425ml vegetable stock, made with 1 stock cube and
>   boiling water
>   100g raisins
>   100g ready-to-eat apricots, chopped
>   50g toasted flaked almonds
>   juice of 1 lemon
>   juice of 1 lime
>   3 tablespoons chopped coriander
>   salt and black pepper

Method
Place the couscous in a bowl and pour on the hot stock.
Leave to stand for 20 minutes until the stock is absorbed. Mix
in the rest of the ingredients, season and serve.

Italian Tuna and Bean Salad
Serves 8
✳ ☉

Ingredients
- 4 tablespoons (60ml) olive oil
- 2 onions, sliced into rings
- 1 tablespoon (15ml) white wine vinegar
- 1 clove garlic, crushed
- 3 × 400g cans cannellini beans, drained
- 2 × 185g cans tuna, drained and flaked
- salt and black pepper

Method
Heat 1 tablespoon (15ml) of the oil and fry the onions until soft and starting to brown. Put the rest of the oil and the vinegar and garlic in a screw-top jar and shake well. Gently mix together the onions, beans and tuna. Drizzle with the dressing, season well and serve.

Mushrooms à la Grecque
Serves 8
※ ◔ **V Ve**

Ingredients
>   8 tablespoons (120ml) olive oil
>   2 large onions, sliced
>   2 cloves garlic, crushed
>   600g economy mushrooms
>   8 tomatoes, cut into wedges
>   100g stoned black olives
>   2 tablespoons (30ml) white wine vinegar
>   salt and black pepper

Method
Heat 2 tablespoons (30ml) of the oil and fry the onions and garlic until soft and starting to brown. Add the mushrooms and tomatoes and gently stir-fry until just softening. Place in a serving dish and garnish with the olives. Mix the rest of the oil with the vinegar, season and drizzle over the salad.

Roasted Pepper Salad
Serves 8
✳ **V Ve**

Ingredients
 8 peppers of mixed colours, deseeded and sliced
 2 cloves garlic, crushed
 6 tablespoons (90ml) olive oil
 salt and black pepper

Method
Preheat the oven to 220°C/425°F/Gas 7. Mix together all the ingredients and season. Roast in the preheated oven for 35 minutes. Transfer with all the juices from the tray to a serving dish and leave to cool.

Main dishes

Stuffed Peppers
Serves 8
V Ve

Ingredients
   2 tablespoons (30ml) oil
   1 large onion, finely chopped
   2 cloves garlic, crushed
   100g mushrooms, finely chopped
   225g bulgar wheat
   1 teaspoon cinnamon
   3 heaped tablespoons raisins
   400ml vegetable stock, made with 1 stock cube and
      boiling water
   salt and pepper
   4 red peppers, deseeded and halved lengthways

Method
Heat 1 tablespoon (15ml) of the oil and fry the onion and
garlic for a few minutes until starting to brown. Add the
mushrooms and stir-fry for 2 minutes, then add all the other
ingredients except the peppers and the remaining oil, stir
well and bring to the boil. Cover tightly and simmer for 30
minutes until the stock has been absorbed. Preheat the oven
to 180°C/350°F/Gas 4. Place the halved peppers in a shallow
ovenproof dish and use the cooked bulgar wheat mixture to
stuff them. Drizzle the remaining oil over the stuffed peppers.
Cover tightly and bake in the preheated oven for 35 minutes.

Sticky Fingers Chicken
Serves 8

Ingredients
>8 tablespoons (120ml) tomato ketchup
>4 tablespoons (60ml) Worcestershire sauce
>4 tablespoons (60ml) light soy sauce
>2 tablespoons (30ml) runny honey
>8 chicken drumsticks
>8 chicken thighs

Method
Preheat the oven to 200°C/400°F/Gas 6. Mix together the tomato ketchup, Worcestershire sauce, soy sauce and honey, then use to coat the chicken pieces. Lay the coated chicken in a single layer on a baking tin. Bake in the preheated oven for 35 minutes until cooked and starting to blacken at the edges.

Chicken and Chick Pea Stew
Serves 8

Ingredients
    3 tablespoons (45ml) oil
    8 chicken thighs
    8 chicken drumsticks
    2 large onions, chopped
    4 cloves garlic, crushed
    500g jar passata (sieved tomatoes)
    2 teaspoons dried thyme
    400g can chick peas, drained
    salt and black pepper

Method
Preheat the oven to 190°C/375°F/Gas 5. Heat half the oil and quickly fry 8 chicken pieces at a time. As each batch is browned, place in an ovenproof dish. Fry the onions in the rest of the oil until starting to brown, then add to the dish. Add the rest of the ingredients and season. Cover and cook in the preheated oven for 1 hour.

Niçoise Salad
Serves 8
✳ ☉

Ingredients

For the salad
    4 eggs
    12 tomatoes, cut into wedges
    2 green peppers, deseeded and cut into thin rings
    1 cucumber, peeled and thinly sliced
    300g can broad beans, drained
    2 × 185g cans tuna, drained and flaked
    2 × 50g cans anchovy fillets, drained
    200g black olives

For the dressing
    8 tablespoons (120ml) olive oil
    3 tablespoons (45ml) white wine vinegar
    2 cloves garlic, crushed
    salt and pepper

Method
Place the eggs in a saucepan, cover with cold water and bring to the boil. Cook for 10 minutes. Plunge into cold water to cool. Peel off the shells and cut each in half lengthways. Arrange all the salad ingredients in a serving dish. Put the oil, vinegar and garlic in a screw-top jar and season. Shake well, then pour over the salad.

Jambalaya
Serves 12

Ingredients
  4 tablespoons (60ml) oil
  4 medium chicken breasts, boned and skinned, cut
     into cubes
  150g chorizo sausage, skinned and sliced
  1 tablespoon paprika
  2 large onions, chopped
  4 celery sticks, sliced
  3 peppers of mixed colours, deseeded and cubed
  4 cloves garlic, crushed
  2 teaspoons (10ml) minced chilli
  700g long-grain rice
  4 tomatoes, cut into wedges
  2 litres chicken stock, made with 2 stock cubes and
     boiling water

Method
Heat the oil and fry the chicken, sausage and paprika for a
few minutes until starting to brown. Remove the meat to a
large saucepan. Fry the onions, celery, peppers, garlic and
chilli until soft and starting to brown. Add to the saucepan
and start to heat through. When hot, add the rice and stir
through. Add the tomatoes and stock. Bring to the boil, then
simmer for 15 minutes until the stock is absorbed.

Tip
Although I had a pan large enough to cook this, you may
need to divide it between 2 large pans.

Chilli-dressed Tuna and Roasted Pepper Salad
Serves 8
✳

Ingredients

For the salad
    4 eggs
    Roasted Pepper Salad (page 109)
    2 × 185g cans tuna, drained and flaked
    200g black olives
    2 tablespoons capers

For the dressing
    4 tablespoons (60ml) olive oil
    1 tablespoon (15ml) white wine vinegar
    2 teaspoons (10ml) minced chilli
    2 cloves garlic, crushed
    salt and pepper

Method
Place the eggs in a saucepan, cover with cold water and bring to the boil. Cook for 10 minutes. Plunge into cold water to cool. Peel off the shells and cut each in half lengthways. Pile all the salad ingredients into a serving dish. Put the dressing ingredients into a screw-top jar and shake well, then drizzle all over the salad.

Mediterranean Lemon Chicken with Olives
Serves 8
✳

Ingredients
- 4 tablespoons (60ml) oil
- 8 chicken legs
- 2 large onions, chopped
- 1 litre curried gravy, made with 150g chip shop curry gravy granules
- 4 tablespoons (60ml) runny honey
- 4 lemons, cut into wedges
- 100g stoned black olives
- black pepper

Method
Preheat the oven to 190°C/375°F/Gas 5. In a large heatproof and ovenproof pan, heat the oil and fry the chicken and onions until starting to brown. Add the gravy and honey and bring to the boil. Add the lemons, then cover and bake in the preheated oven for 1 hour. Stir through the olives and season before serving.

5 Something Special

There are certain times when a *dîner à deux* is called for or you want to whip up a special meal for someone's birthday. I have included some out-of-the-ordinary recipes here. They are a little more expensive but still shouldn't break the bank.

For a really simple yet stylish birthday spread for six you could use the recipe for Sabzi Curry (page 119), choose another curry sauce from this range and make a chicken curry, serve them with a salad of sliced onions and tomatoes, rice, some poppadoms and two Indian pickles and you would have a great feast.

There are also some dishes for friends who want to cook a Sunday lunch together. Here are some alternatives to Sunday roasts (which can be expensive). It's easy to produce a baked dish that can be served with some simple veg or salad. Alternatively, there's a curried chicken salad for summer days.

Special Treats

Canoodle Noodles
Serves 2
🕐 **V**

Ingredients
> 125g medium egg noodles
> 1 tablespoon (15ml) oil
> 1 red pepper, deseeded and sliced
> 200g broccoli, broken into small florets
> 100g chestnut mushrooms, sliced
> 50g cashew nuts
> 1 teaspoon (5ml) minced ginger
> 1 tablespoon (15ml) soy sauce
> 1 tablespoon (15ml) runny honey

Method
Cook the noodles in boiling water for 4 minutes, then drain.
Meanwhile, preheat the grill and line the grill tray with foil.
Heat the oil and stir-fry the pepper, broccoli and mushrooms
for 3 minutes. Grill the cashews until starting to brown – but
don't burn them! Add the ginger, soy sauce and honey to the
stir-fry and stir through. Mix together all the ingredients and
serve.

Sabzi Curry

Serves 2–3

✳ ◔ **V**

Ingredients

    1 tablespoon (15ml) oil
    1 onion, thinly sliced
    225g okra, washed and stalk ends cut off
    100g mushrooms, sliced
    350g jar Madhur Jaffrey's sabzi sauce
    250g spinach, large stalks removed and roughly
       chopped

Method

Heat the oil and fry the onion for 2–3 minutes. If the okra are quite long, cut the stems in two about halfway down. Add the okra to the onion and fry for another 4–5 minutes. Add the mushrooms and stir-fry for another minute. Add the sabzi sauce and bring to the boil, stirring well. Reduce the heat, cover and simmer for 3 minutes. Add the spinach and keep stirring until it has wilted into the curry, then serve.

Tip

For a special occasion, this is wonderful served with rice, naan breads and Indian salads accompanied by wedges of lemons and limes and a couple of Indian pickles such as brinjal and tomato.

Coconut Chicken Curry
Serves 2
❋

Ingredients
>   1 tablespoon (15ml) oil
>   1 onion, diced
>   ½ green pepper, deseeded and diced
>   350g chicken thighs, skinned
>   100g mushrooms, quartered
>   2 tablespoons (30ml) medium balti curry paste
>   1 teaspoon (5ml) minced lemongrass
>   1 teaspoon (5ml) minced ginger
>   2 cloves garlic, crushed
>   1 tablespoon (15ml) soy sauce
>   200ml carton coconut cream
>   handful of basil leaves (optional)

Method
Heat the oil and fry the onion and pepper for 5–10 minutes until starting to brown. Add the chicken thighs and fry for another 5 minutes. Add the mushrooms, curry paste, lemongrass, ginger, garlic and soy sauce and stir-fry for 2–3 minutes. Add the coconut cream, stir well, cover and simmer for 5 minutes. Stir in the basil (if using) just before serving.

Tip
Serve with rice and a side salad of tomatoes and onion or spinach salad.

West Country Chicken
Serves 2
✳

Ingredients
> 25g butter, softened
> 2 tablespoons (30ml) whole-grain mustard
> 1 teaspoon (5ml) Worcestershire sauce (optional)
> 2 medium chicken breasts
> 1 apple, cored, peeled and sliced
> ¼ Savoy cabbage, sliced
> 250ml bottle dry cider

Method
Preheat the oven to 190°C/375°F/Gas 5. Combine the butter, mustard and Worcestershire sauce (if using) and use this to coat the chicken breasts. Put the apple and cabbage in an ovenproof dish and place the chicken breasts on top. Pour over the cider, cover and cook in the preheated oven for 50 minutes.

Roasted Coconut Chicken
Serves 4
✳

Ingredients
    2 tablespoons (30ml) medium balti curry paste
    2 tablespoons (30ml) oil
    1 teaspoon (5ml) minced ginger
    1 teaspoon (5ml) minced lemongrass or finely chopped
      fresh lemongrass
    400g can coconut milk
    1.5kg free-range chicken

Method
Preheat the oven to 190°C/375°F/Gas 5. Mix together the curry paste, oil, ginger and lemongrass with 2 tablespoons (30ml) of the coconut milk. Brush the chicken all over with the paste and place any remaining paste inside the chicken. Put the chicken in a roasting tin and pour over the remaining coconut milk. Roast in the preheated oven for 1½ hours, basting occasionally with the coconut milk. When the chicken is cooked, leave to stand for 10 minutes before carving. To check the chicken is cooked, stick a sharp knife into the thigh and make sure that the juices are running clear. Any sign of pink in the juices means that the chicken needs to be cooked a little longer.

Kebabs with Satay Sauce
Serves 4

Ingredients

For the kebabs
    2 tablespoons (30ml) medium balti curry paste
    1 tablespoon (15ml) soy sauce
    1 teaspoon (5ml) honey or sugar
    500g lean flash-fry steak, cubed

For the satay sauce
    100g crunchy peanut butter
    200ml carton creamed coconut
    1 tablespoon (15ml) lemon juice
    1/2 teaspoon (2.5ml) minced chilli

Method
Mix together the curry paste, soy sauce and honey or sugar.
Add the steak and marinate for 1 hour. Preheat the grill.
Thread the meat on to 8 wooden skewers. Grill the kebabs
for 8 minutes, turning once. Meanwhile, mix together the
sauce ingredients and heat gently, stirring until well combined.

Moroccan Meatballs with Gravy and Vegetables
Serves 6

Ingredients
   2 small onions, finely chopped
   1 heaped tablespoon raisins
   750g minced beef
   1 tablespoon (15ml) tomato purée
   1 teaspoon curry powder
   3 tablespoons (45ml) oil
   ½ teaspoon cinnamon
   600ml curried gravy, made with 100g chip shop curry
      gravy granules
   juice of ½ lemon
   2 celery sticks, thickly sliced
   1 large or 2 medium courgettes, sliced
   180g frozen peas

Method
Mix together half the onion, the raisins, beef, tomato purée
and curry powder. Shape the mixture into 24 meatballs.
Using 1 tablespoon (15ml) of the oil, fry the meatballs in
small batches, until browned. Tip out the excess fat and put
all the meatballs in the pan. Add the cinnamon, gravy and
lemon juice, cover and cook for 25–30 minutes until the
meatballs are cooked. Heat the remaining 2 tablespoons
(30ml) of oil and fry the celery and courgettes until soft and
starting to brown. Add the peas and continue cooking for 5
minutes until the peas are cooked. Just before serving stir the
vegetables into the meatballs and gravy.

Tip
You could omit the cinnamon but it is this that gives it a
Moroccan flavour.

Lime-fried Chicken
Serves 6
✳ ⏲

Ingredients
>   3 tablespoons (45ml) oil
>   4 medium chicken breasts, boned and skinned, cut
>   into bite-sized pieces
>   1 onion, chopped
>   2 cloves garlic, crushed
>   grated zest and juice of 2 limes
>   15g pack coriander, chopped

Method
Heat the oil and fry the chicken, onion and garlic for about 10 minutes until starting to brown. Add the lime zest and juice and coriander and stir-fry for 1 minute, then serve.

Potato Moussaka
Serves 4–6

Ingredients
>   1kg potatoes

For the meat sauce
>   2 tablespoons (30ml) oil
>   2 onions, chopped
>   2 cloves garlic, crushed
>   500g minced lamb
>   1 teaspoon ground cinnamon
>   400g can chopped tomatoes
>   1 teaspoon (5ml) honey or sugar
>   1 teaspoon oregano
>   2 tablespoons (30ml) tomato purée
>   salt and black pepper

For the cheese topping
>   3 eggs, beaten
>   150g natural yogurt
>   200g cheese, grated

Method
Boil the potatoes for 10 minutes, then slice thickly. Heat the oil and fry the onions and garlic until starting to brown. Add the lamb and cinnamon and stir-fry until the meat is browned. Add the rest of the ingredients for the meat sauce and simmer gently for 15 minutes. Meanwhile, preheat the oven to 200°C/400°F/Gas 6. Place a layer of potatoes in an ovenproof dish, then cover with alternate layers of meat sauce and potatoes, finishing with a meat layer. Beat together the eggs, yogurt and half the cheese and spoon this over the meat layer. Sprinkle with the remaining cheese and cook, uncovered, in the preheated oven for 40 minutes.

X-tra Nice Chicken
Serves 6

Ingredients
> 2 tablespoons (30ml) oil
> 6 medium chicken breasts, boned and skinned
> knob of butter
> 6 tomatoes, chopped
> 3 tablespoons (45ml) whole-grain mustard
> 150ml white wine or chicken stock, made with 1 stock
> cube and boiling water
> 2 tablespoons fresh tarragon, chopped
> salt and black pepper
> 100ml crème fraîche

Method
Preheat the oven to 180°C/350°F/Gas 4. Heat the oil and fry the chicken until browned. Place in an ovenproof dish. Add the butter to the pan and fry the tomatoes for 3 minutes. Stir in the mustard and wine or stock, bring to the boil and pour over the chicken. Sprinkle with the tarragon, season, then cover and cook for 35 minutes. Stir in the crème fraîche just before serving.

Tip
You can use chopped tarragon in a cheese and herb omelette.

Sunday Lunches

Pot-roasted Chicken
Serves 4
❋

Ingredients
    ½ Savoy cabbage, sliced
    1 large leek, sliced
    1.7–2kg free-range chicken
    1 chicken stock cube
    sprinkling of dried thyme
    25g butter

Method
Preheat the oven to 200°C/400°F/Gas 6. Put the cabbage and leek in a large casserole dish and place the chicken on top. Make up the stock cube with 300ml boiling water, then add the thyme. Pour the stock over the chicken and dot with pieces of butter. Cover and cook in the preheated oven for 1 hour. Remove the cover and cook for another 30 minutes. Divide the chicken and vegetables between 4 plates, spoon over the cooking liquid and serve.

Tip
This is best served with baking potatoes which have the bonus of being cooked alongside the chicken.

If you don't have a casserole dish use a roasting tin and cover it with roasting foil.

Winter Warmer
Serves 4–6

Ingredients
>700g potatoes, thickly sliced
>1 tablespoon (15ml) oil
>2 onions, peeled and cut into rings
>1 tablespoon demerara sugar
>1 teaspoon (5ml) white wine vinegar
>2 × 400g cans frankfurters, drained and sliced
>400g can butter beans, drained
>2 tablespoons (30ml) whole-grain mustard
>200ml crème fraîche

Method
Preheat the oven to 190°C/375°F/Gas 5. Cook the potatoes in boiling water for just 5 minutes, then drain well. Meanwhile, heat the oil and fry the onions for a few minutes until soft and starting to brown. Add the sugar and vinegar and continue to cook until a deep brown colour. Mix together the onions, frankfurters, butter beans, mustard and 4 tablespoons of the crème fraîche and place in an ovenproof dish. Cover with the potato slices and spoon over the rest of the crème fraîche. Bake in the preheated oven for 50 minutes until the top is golden brown.

Veggie Winter Warmer
Serves 4–6
V

Ingredients
700g potatoes, thickly sliced
2 tablespoons (30ml) oil
2 onions, chopped
560g veggie sausages, defrosted and cut into chunks
2 × 400g cans chilli beans
200ml vegetable stock, made with 1 stock cube and
    boiling water
1 tablespoon (15ml) whole-grain mustard
50g butter
salt and black pepper

Method
Preheat the oven to 190°C/375°F/Gas 5. Boil the potatoes for 5 minutes, then drain well. Heat the oil and fry the onions and sausages until starting to brown. Mix together the onions, sausages, chilli beans and stock and place in a shallow ovenproof dish. Cover with the potatoes. Mix together the mustard and butter and spoon over the potatoes. Season. Bake, uncovered, in the preheated oven for 50 minutes.

Vegetarian Pasta Bake
Serves 6
V

Ingredients
    4 tablespoons (60ml) oil
    1 onion, chopped
    3 peppers of mixed colours, deseeded and cubed
    2 courgettes, halved and sliced
    250g mushrooms, sliced
    400g can chopped tomatoes
    1 tablespoon (15ml) tomato purée
    4 sun-dried tomatoes, sliced
    1 teaspoon dried oregano
    salt and pepper
    300g penne pasta
    350ml ready-made cheese sauce
    50g Cheddar cheese, grated

Method
Preheat the oven to 190°C/375°F/Gas 5. Heat the oil and fry the onion for about 5 minutes until starting to brown. Add the peppers, courgettes and mushrooms and fry for another 10 minutes. Add the tomatoes, tomato purée, sun-dried tomatoes and oregano. Season and simmer for 10 minutes. Meanwhile, cook the pasta in boiling water according to the packet instructions, then drain. Put the sauced vegetables in a large ovenproof dish. Mix the pasta with the cheese sauce and spoon over the vegetables. Sprinkle with the cheese and bake in the preheated oven for 25 minutes until golden brown on top.

Garlic Chicken
Serves 6

Ingredients
  6 chicken legs
  1 tablespoon (15ml) oil
  1 onion, diced
  3 tablespoons (45ml) white wine vinegar
  400g can chopped tomatoes
  4 cloves garlic, crushed
  1 tablespoon paprika
  ½ teaspoon dried thyme
  salt and black pepper
  100ml crème fraîche

Method
Preheat the oven to 180°C/350°F/Gas 4. Put the chicken in a large ovenproof tin or casserole dish. Heat the oil and fry the onion until just starting to brown. Add with the rest of the ingredients, except the crème fraîche, to the chicken. Season, cover with a tightly fitting lid or foil and cook in the preheated oven for 55 minutes. Stir in the crème fraîche just before serving.

Spinach and Red Pesto Bake
Serves 6
V

Ingredients
> 225g baby spinach
> 142ml carton double cream
> salt and black pepper
> 6 slices white bread, crusts removed and sliced
>   diagonally
> 175g jar red pesto sauce
> 250g Cheddar cheese, grated
> 3 eggs, beaten
> 450ml milk

Method
Preheat the oven to 190°C/375°F/Gas 5. Cook the spinach in boiling water for a few minutes to wilt it, then drain well and squeeze out as much water as you can. Mix with the cream and season. Use 2 slices of bread to cover the bottom of an ovenproof dish. Spoon in half the red pesto sauce, spread over the bread and cover with half the creamed spinach. Sprinkle with one-third of the cheese. Cover with 2 more slices of bread and spread these with the remaining red pesto sauce, the remaining creamed spinach and half the remaining cheese. Top with the last 2 slices of bread. Mix together the eggs and milk and season. Pour over the bread, then sprinkle with the remaining cheese. Bake in the preheated oven for 35 minutes.

Tip
You can vary this bake by substituting other sauces for the red pesto. We made a lovely one with an aubergine and pepper sauce.

Roasted Chicken and Vegetables
Serves 6

Ingredients
- 6 chicken drumsticks
- 6 chicken thighs
- salt and black pepper
- 3 peppers of mixed colours, deseeded and cut into strips
- 450g sweet potatoes, cut into small chips
- 2 tablespoons (30ml) oil
- 200ml chicken stock, made with 1 stock cube and boiling water
- 2 cloves garlic, crushed
- 1 tablespoon (15ml) tomato purée
- 3 tomatoes, halved
- 2 slices bread, crumbed
- 1 bunch of green parsley, finely chopped

Method
Preheat the oven to 190°C/375°F/Gas 5. Put the chicken pieces in a large roasting tin and season. Place the peppers and potatoes in a large bowl and add the oil. Mix well so all the vegetables have a coating of oil, then season and place in the roasting tin. Roast the chicken and vegetables in the preheated oven for 50 minutes. Mix together the hot stock, garlic and tomato purée and pour over the chicken and vegetables. Place the tomatoes in the tin, mix together the breadcrumbs and parsley and sprinkle over the dish. Return to the oven for 15 minutes until the topping has browned. Serve.

Tip
The parsley is an integral ingredient in this dish, not a garnish. You can buy it pre-chopped now if you wish, but this is more expensive.

Coronation Chicken Salad
Serves 6
※ ☉

Ingredients

    4 roasted chicken breasts, skin removed and meat cut
        into strips
    300g jar coronation dressing
    3 bananas, sliced
    50g ready-to-eat apricots, diced
    1 heaped tablespoon raisins
    1 bunch of spring onions, sliced
    1 bunch of watercress
    iceberg lettuce leaves, shredded
    salt and black pepper

Method

Mix together the chicken, dressing, bananas, apricots and raisins. Place the spring onions, watercress and lettuce in a serving dish. Spoon the coronation chicken on to the salad. Season and serve.

6 Simple Budget Standbys

These are some of the cheapest recipes in the book. When your money is running out these are the ones to turn to. Here also is a survival guide that will ensure that you have a healthy diet even when you are reduced to trying to live on a pittance. Don't forget to claim any customer loyalty card tokens or vouchers if you've been shopping at the same supermarket regularly. Canny students will have signed up with a friend at the beginning of term to one of the supermarket loyalty schemes to ensure they have maximised their returns.

Survival Guide

Shopping list

2 × 1 litre economy cartons of orange juice
2.27 litres milk
300g Cheddar cheese
250g butter (use sparingly in sandwiches and substitute
    for oil in cooking)
½ dozen free-range eggs
125g tub soft cheese with garlic
1 large loaf bread
6 tomatoes
½ cucumber
3 onions
100g mushrooms
2 chillis
1 small leek
1 small courgette
225g broccoli
1 large baking potato
900g apples   ⎫
900g bananas ⎬ 14 pieces of fruit in total
           ⎭
750g economy branflakes
400g can economy tomatoes
400g can economy baked beans
400g can economy red kidney beans
500g packet economy pasta

This presupposes that your stock cupboard holds only salt and black pepper, which hopefully isn't true.

Meal Plan

Breakfast each day
Branflakes and milk, orange juice

Lunch each day
Sandwich of grated cheese and cucumber or sliced tomato
Banana or apple

Evening meals
Student Standby (page 140) and pasta
Creamed Leek and Courgette Sauce (page 142) and pasta
Omelette (page 144) with cheese and tomato, 2 slices bread
Broccoli Sauce (page 142) and pasta
2 scrambled eggs (page 195), baked beans and 2 slices toast
Chilli and Garlic Beans (page 141) with a baked potato

Serve orange juice with the evening meal and follow with another apple or banana. This will ensure you a healthy diet, but this is fairly restrictive and would need to be varied over a period of time.

Student Standby
Serves 1
✳ ☉ **V**

Ingredients
    1 tablespoon (15ml) oil
    1 onion, chopped
    1 clove garlic, crushed (optional)
    100g mushrooms, sliced
    1 tomato, cut into wedges
    25g cheese, grated
    salt and black pepper

Method
Heat the oil and fry the onion, garlic and mushrooms until soft and starting to brown. Add the tomato and cook for a few minutes until just softening. Stir in the cheese, season and serve.

Tip
Use as a topping for pasta.

Chilli and Garlic Beans
Serves 1
✳ ◷ **V**

Ingredients
      1 tablespoon (15ml) oil
      1 onion, thinly sliced
      1 chilli, deseeded and finely chopped
      35g soft cheese with garlic
      400g can economy red kidney beans, drained

Method
Heat the oil and fry the onion until soft and starting to brown.
Add the rest of the ingredients and continue cooking until the
cheese melts down into a sauce.

Tip
Serve over pasta or with a baked potato.

Creamed Leek and Courgette Sauce
(for pasta)
Serves 1
✳ ◔ **V**

Ingredients
    1 tablespoon (15ml) oil
    1 small leek, thinly sliced
    1 small courgette, thinly sliced
    40g soft cheese with garlic
    black pepper

Method
Heat the oil and fry the leek and courgette until soft and starting to brown. Add the cheese and melt down until you have a creamy sauce. Season and serve on your favourite pasta.

Tip
You can also use this recipe to make a Broccoli Sauce for pasta. Just substitute an onion for the leek and 225g cooked broccoli for the courgette.

Chick Peas and Veg
Serves 2
✳ ◷ **V**

Ingredients
>   1 tablespoon (15ml) oil
>   1 onion, chopped
>   1 courgette, halved and sliced
>   40g soft cheese with garlic
>   400g can chick peas, drained

Method
Heat the oil and fry the onion and courgette until soft and starting to brown. Add the cheese and melt down to a sauce. Stir in the chick peas and serve.

Tip
Use as a topping for baked potatoes or pasta.

Omelette *(cheese and tomato)*
Serves 2
✳ ◕ **V**

Ingredients
    4 eggs, beaten
    salt and black pepper
    1 tablespoon (15ml) oil
    50g cheese, grated
    2 tomatoes, chopped

Method
Season the eggs. Heat the oil in a frying pan, pour in the eggs and keep drawing the edges of the omelette from the sides of the pan so that uncooked egg can run underneath. The omelette should only take 2–3 minutes to set. Add the cheese and tomatoes and fold in half. Slide the omelette on to a dish, cut in half and serve.

Tip
You can vary the toppings using whatever you have in the fridge. Cooked mushrooms and broccoli make a good filling, or chopped ham (with or without grated cheese). To make an omelette for one person, just halve the ingredients.

Tikka Masala Sauce
Serves 2
※ ☉ **V**

Ingredients
    1 tablespoon (15ml) oil
    1 onion, chopped
    2 cloves garlic, crushed
    2 tablespoons (30ml) tikka seasoning
    150g carton natural yogurt
    142ml carton double cream

Method
Heat the oil and fry the onion and garlic until soft and starting to brown. Stir in the tikka seasoning and cook for 1 minute. Add the yogurt and cream and heat gently.

Tip
Use to cover cooked chicken or a mixture of cooked vegetables or warmed canned beans.

Spaghetti Tunagnese
Serves 2
🕒

Ingredients
150g spaghetti
142ml carton single cream
25g Cheddar cheese, finely grated
100g can tuna, drained and flaked
salt
Worcestershire sauce to taste (optional)
½ bunch of spring onions, chopped

Method
Cook the spaghetti in a large saucepan of boiling water according to the packet instructions, then drain. Put the cream in a small milkpan and bring to the boil, then gently simmer for 5 minutes. Take the cream off the heat and add the cheese, blending well to make a smooth sauce. Add the rest of the ingredients and heat through gently. Serve with the spaghetti.

Tip
This is even more delicious if topped with shavings of Parmesan cheese (use a potato peeler) and some freshly ground black pepper.

Vegetables in Creamy Mustard Sauce with Chorizo
Serves 2
✳ ⏲

Ingredients
  2 tablespoons (30ml) oil
  1 onion, chopped
  225g potatoes, peeled and thinly sliced
  2 carrots, peeled and thinly sliced
  300ml vegetable stock, made with 1 stock cube and
    boiling water
  142ml carton single cream
  1 dessertspoon (10ml) whole-grain mustard
  50g chorizo sausage, thinly sliced
  salt and black pepper

Method
Heat the oil and fry the onion and potatoes for a few minutes
until softening and starting to brown. Add the carrots and
stock, cover tightly and cook for 20 minutes until the
vegetables are cooked. Just before serving, stir in the other
ingredients, season, warm through and serve.

Tip
Serve with rice.

Other cooked sausages can be substituted for the chorizo.

Eggs Florentine
Serves 3
✳ ⊙ **V**

Ingredients
>   250g spinach
>   50ml crème fraîche
>   black pepper
>   1 tablespoon (15ml) oil
>   6 eggs

Method
Wash the spinach and place in a large saucepan with 3 tablespoons (45ml) of water. Turn up the heat and cook for 2–3 minutes until the spinach has wilted down. Stir in the crème fraîche, season and keep warm while you heat the oil and fry the eggs. Serve the eggs on the spinach.

Tip
Serve with pasta or rice.

Vegetable and Lentil Soup
Serves 4
* **V Ve**

Ingredients
>   500g potatoes, peeled and diced
>   1 carrot, halved and sliced
>   1 onion, chopped
>   1.2 litres vegetable stock, made with 2 stock cubes
>   and boiling water
>   400g can lentils, drained

Method
Put all the ingredients in a large saucepan and bring to the boil. Cover and simmer for 25 minutes. Squash some of the vegetables against the side of the saucepan to thicken the soup a little. Serve with crusty bread.

Mascarpone and Tomato Sauce
(for pasta)
Serves 4
✳ ⏲ **V**

Ingredients
    1 tablespoon (15ml) oil
    1 onion, chopped
    2 cloves garlic, crushed
    500g jar passata (sieved tomatoes)
    100g mascarpone cheese
    black pepper

Method
Heat the oil and fry the onion and garlic until browned. Add
the passata and simmer for 4 minutes. Stir in the mascarpone
and keep stirring until it has been incorporated into the
sauce. Season and serve mixed into your favourite pasta.

Tip
I sometimes add some sliced sun-dried tomatoes to this when
I add the passata.

Tomato, Leek and Bacon Rice
Serves 4
✳ ◔

Ingredients
 2 tablespoons (30ml) oil
 2 large leeks, sliced
 1 clove garlic, crushed
 125g bacon, chopped
 400g can chopped tomatoes
 250g long-grain rice
 700ml chicken stock, made with 1 stock cube and
  boiling water
 black pepper

Method
Heat the oil and fry the leeks, garlic and bacon for a few
minutes until soft and starting to brown. Add the tomatoes
and rice and cook for 1 minute. Add the stock, season and
cook until the rice is cooked and the stock absorbed. Stir and
serve immediately.

Bean Paprikash
Serves 4
✳ ☉ **V**

Ingredients
>1 tablespoon (15ml) oil
>2 onions, chopped
>2 dessertspoons paprika
>200ml carton crème fraîche
>400g can economy baked beans
>400g can economy red kidney beans, drained
>salt and black pepper

Method
Heat the oil and fry the onions until soft and browned. Add the paprika and crème fraîche. Gently simmer for 5 minutes, then stir in both types of beans. Heat through, season and serve.

Lebanese Salad
Serves 4
V Ve

Ingredients
>100g Puy lentils
>1 tablespoon (15ml) tomato purée
>1½ pints (800ml) vegetable stock, made with 1 stock
> cube and boiling water
>100g bulgar wheat
>juice of 1 lemon
>salt and black pepper
>1 tablespoon (15ml) oil
>2 onions, sliced
>1 teaspoon sugar
>1 bunch of fresh mint, chopped
>3 tomatoes, cut into wedges

Method
Put the lentils, tomato purée and stock in a pan and bring to the boil. Cover tightly and simmer for 20 minutes. Add the bulgar wheat and lemon juice and season. Cook for 10 minutes until the stock has been absorbed. Meanwhile, heat the oil and fry the onions and sugar until deep brown and caramelised. Stir the mint into the lentil and bulgar wheat mixture. Serve the salad topped with the fried onions and tomato wedges.

Tip
You can also make this substituting coriander for the mint.

Aubergines Baked with Cheese
Serves 4
V

Ingredients
    2 aubergines, sliced in half lengthways
    3 tablespoons (45ml) olive oil
    1 onion, chopped
    1 clove garlic, crushed
    220g can chopped tomatoes
    1 tablespoon (15ml) tomato purée
    100g mozzarella cheese, cut into 8 thin slices
    black pepper

Method
Preheat the oven to 200°C/400°F/Gas 6. Coat the aubergines with 2 tablespoons (30ml) of the oil and place on a baking tray. Roast in the preheated oven for 25 minutes. Meanwhile, fry the onion and garlic in the remaining oil until soft and starting to brown. Add the tomatoes and tomato purée and simmer for approximately 5–10 minutes until the sauce has thickened. Remove the aubergines from the oven and cover each half with some sauce and 2 of the cheese slices. Season and return to the oven for 10–15 minutes to melt the cheese.

Mascarpone Macaroni Cheese
Serves 4
🕐 **V**

Ingredients
    250g quick-cook macaroni
    100g mascarpone cheese
    100ml milk
    2 teaspoons (10ml) Dijon mustard
    salt and black pepper
    100g cheese, grated

Method
Cook the macaroni in boiling water according to the packet instructions, then drain. Meanwhile, gently heat the mascarpone, milk and mustard until melted into a sauce. Season with salt and black pepper. Serve the macaroni with the cheese sauce spooned over and sprinkled with the cheese.

Potato and Tomato Curry
Serves 4
✳ ⏲ **V Ve**

Ingredients
    2 tablespoons (30ml) oil
    2 onions, chopped
    2 cloves garlic, crushed
    700g potatoes, peeled and cubed
    4 tablespoons medium curry powder
    6 tomatoes, cut into wedges
    300ml vegetable stock, made with 1 stock cube and
        boiling water

Method
Heat the oil and fry the onions and garlic until starting to brown. Add the potatoes and curry powder, stir in, then add the tomatoes and stock. Bring to the boil, cover tightly and simmer for 20–25 minutes until the potatoes are cooked.

Pasta with Roasted Veg
Serves 4
V Ve

Ingredients
> 800g mixed vegetables including red pepper, onion,
>   courgettes, mushrooms, tomatoes
> 1 clove garlic, crushed
> sprinkling of dried thyme
> oil
> 350g pasta – bows or spirals are very good

Method
Preheat the oven to its highest temperature. Slice, halve or
roughly dice the vegetables. Put them in a bowl with the
garlic and thyme and use just enough oil to coat them all.
Transfer to a roasting sheet and cook, uncovered, in the
preheated oven for 30–40 minutes until soft and blackening
at the edges. Meanwhile, cook the pasta according to the
packet instructions. Drain the pasta and serve topped with
the roasted vegetables.

Tip
Non-vegans can add some grated cheese to the finished dish.

One-pan Ratatouille
Serves 6
✳ ⊕ **V Ve**

Ingredients
        100ml oil
        2 onions, chopped
        1 aubergine, halved and sliced
        2 large courgettes, halved and sliced
        1 red pepper, deseeded and cubed
        1 yellow pepper, deseeded and cubed
        2 cloves garlic, crushed
        400g can chopped tomatoes
        salt and black pepper

Method
Heat the oil in a large pan until very hot and stir-fry all the vegetables except the tomatoes for a few minutes. Add the tomatoes, season and stir well. Cover tightly and simmer for 20 minutes until all the vegetables are cooked.

Tip
This is a lot of oil for one dish but the vegetables need this. Since you taste the oil more in the finished dish, the better oil you use, such as olive, the better the finished dish will be.

You can also use this recipe to make Ratatouille Gratin: preheat the grill, transfer the ratatouille to a shallow oven-proof dish and sprinkle with 4 tablespoons white bread-crumbs and 4 tablespoons grated cheese. Grill until the top is golden brown.

Cauliflower Cheese and Bean Gratin
Serves 4
🕐 **V**

Ingredients
  1 small cauliflower, divided into florets
  400g can red kidney beans, drained
  400g can chick peas, drained
  350ml ready-made cheese sauce
  salt and black pepper
  2 tablespoons breadcrumbs
  50g Cheddar cheese, grated

Method
Cook the cauliflower in boiling water for about 10 minutes until tender, then drain. Mix with the beans, chick peas and cheese sauce, season and place in a heatproof dish. Preheat the grill. Mix together the breadcrumbs and cheese and sprinkle over the dish. Grill until the top is bubbling and brown.

7 Etc, Etc . . .

If you want to push the boat out a little, here are some different ways of cooking those staples such as rice, noodles and potato. There's even a recipe for mashed potato and olive oil as seen in a number of trendy restaurants now.

I haven't included many vegetable dishes as most students have to keep their meals simple to save money, but I do recommend the Baked Tomatoes in Cheesy Cream (page 168) as an accompaniment to a simple chicken or meat dish. It really is to die for.

You will also find a couple of desserts for special occasions: a fruit crumble (page 183) to serve after Sunday lunch, Eton Mess (page 184) for a very special dessert that is incredibly easy to make, and a yogurt concoction (page 182) to help use up any bits and pieces in your food store. There is also my simplest version yet of the humble flapjack (page 186) and a easy recipe for rock buns (page 185).

Peanut Butter Sauce
Serves 4
✳ ⏲ **V**

Ingredients
>   6 tablespoons peanut butter
>   6 tablespoons (90ml) water
>   1 tablespoon (15ml) soy sauce
>   2 teaspoons (10ml) runny honey
>   black pepper

Method
In a small saucepan, gently heat all the ingredients until you
have a smooth sauce.

Tip
You can make this with smooth or crunchy peanut butter.

Salad Dressing
Serves 4
✳ ☾ **V Ve**

Ingredients
>   4 tablespoons (60ml) oil
>   1 tablespoon (15ml) white wine vinegar
>   1 teaspoon (5ml) Dijon mustard
>   pinch of caster sugar
>   salt and black pepper

Method
Put all the ingredients in a screw-top jar and shake well.

Mustard-dressed Mixed Salad
Serves 4
✳ ⊙ **V Ve**

Ingredients

For the salad
    1 round lettuce
    100g mushrooms, sliced
    125g packet radishes, sliced
    1 carrot, grated
    1 heaped tablespoon raisins
    1 heaped tablespoon sunflower seeds

For the dressing
    6 tablespoons (90ml) olive oil
    2 tablespoons (30ml) white wine vinegar
    1 clove garlic, crushed
    2 teaspoons (10ml) whole-grain mustard
    1 teaspoon (15ml) Dijon mustard
    salt and black pepper

Method
Combine all the salad ingredients in a large salad bowl. Put all the dressing ingredients in a screw-top jar and shake well, then use to dress the salad.

Stir-fried Greens
Serves 4
✳ ⊙ **V Ve**

Ingredients
>   2 tablespoons (30ml) oil
>   ½ Savoy cabbage, shredded
>   250g spinach, shredded if large leaved
>   2 cloves garlic, crushed
>   2 teaspoons (10ml) minced ginger
>   2 tablespoons (30ml) soy sauce

Method
Heat the oil and stir-fry the cabbage, spinach and garlic until the spinach is just starting to wilt. Add the ginger and soy sauce, stir through and serve.

Tip
This recipe is easily adapted to serve 2 people: just halve the ingredients.

Stir-fried Courgettes
Serves 6
❋ ⊙ **V Ve**

Ingredients
>   3 tablespoons (45ml) oil
>   2 large or 4 medium courgettes, sliced
>   3 garlic cloves, crushed
>   1 bunch of spring onions, sliced
>   salt and black pepper

Method
Heat the oil and fry the courgettes and garlic for 8 minutes until starting to brown. Add the spring onions and stir-fry for another 2 minutes. Season and serve.

Stir-fried Celery and Walnuts
Serves 6
✳ ◷ **V**

Ingredients
    knob of butter
    1 bunch of celery, trimmed and chopped diagonally
    75g walnut pieces
    2 tablespoons demerara sugar

Method
Melt the butter and stir-fry the celery for 2 minutes. Add the walnuts and sugar and stir until the sugar caramelises.

Tip
This is excellent as an accompaniment to any roasted or grilled meats or poultry.

Baked Tomatoes in Cheesy Cream
Serves 6
✳ **V**

Ingredients
>   500g small tomatoes, halved
>   100g Gruyère cheese, grated
>   284ml carton whipping cream
>   black pepper

Method
Preheat the oven to 190°C/375°F/Gas 5. Arrange the tomatoes in a shallow ovenproof dish, cut side uppermost. Sprinkle with the cheese and pour over the cream. Season and bake in the preheated oven for 35 minutes until starting to brown. These are best served warm.

Tip
Tuck some fresh herbs in with the tomatoes, if you have some.

You can use this as a main course for 2–3 people if you serve it with some bread or rice.

Wedgy Potatoes
Serves 2
 ✳ **V Ve**

Ingredients
> 2 large potatoes
> 2 tablespoons (30ml) oil
> $1/2$ teaspoon paprika
> 1 clove garlic, crushed
> salt and pepper

Method
Preheat the oven to 200°C/400°F/Gas 6. Cut each potato into 8 wedges. Put all the ingredients into a bowl and stir thoroughly to ensure the potato wedges are covered with oil. Tip on to a roasting tray and cook in the preheated oven for 45 minutes until browned and cooked through.

Tip
These make a change from jacket potatoes and also make a tasty snack when served with a dip and some salad.

Roasted New Potatoes
Serves 4
* **V Ve**

Ingredients
    450g new potatoes, unpeeled
    2 tablespoons (30ml) oil
    1 clove garlic, crushed
    1 tablespoon chopped fresh parsley (optional)
    salt and black pepper

Method
Preheat the oven to 180°C/350°F/Gas 4. Cook the potatoes in boiling water for 5 minutes, then drain well. Mix together all the ingredients in a bowl, so that all are well covered in oil. Tip the contents of the bowl on to a baking tray and roast for 30 minutes until the potatoes are well browned.

Tip
Other herbs such as basil or rosemary could be substituted for the parsley.

Mashed Potato with Garlic and Olive Oil
Serves 6
✳ ☽ **V Ve**

Ingredients
>700g potatoes, peeled and cut into chunks
>10 tablespoons (150ml) olive oil
>juice of ½ lemon
>2 cloves garlic, crushed
>salt and black pepper

Method
Cook the potatoes in boiling water until tender (about 15–20 minutes), then drain well. Mash with a potato masher or fork. Gradually add the other ingredients and work them in. Season and serve.

Tomato and Sweet Potato Gratin
Serves 6
✳ **V**

Ingredients
1 tablespoon (15ml) oil
500g tomatoes, sliced
500g sweet potatoes, sliced
pinch of dried oregano
50g Gruyère cheese, grated
salt and pepper

Method
Preheat the oven to 190°C/375°F/Gas 5. Place the oil, tomatoes and potatoes in a large ovenproof dish. Cover tightly and bake in the preheated oven for 1 hour. Remove the cover, sprinkle with the oregano and cheese, season and bake, uncovered, for another 20 minutes until brown on top.

Swedish Anchovy Potato Pie
Serves 6

Ingredients
>2 tablespoons (30ml) oil
>2 onions, sliced
>50g can anchovy fillets, drained
>284ml carton whipping cream
>150ml milk
>1kg potatoes, peeled and cut into small matchsticks
>black pepper

Method
Preheat the oven to 190°C/375°F/Gas 5. Heat the oil and fry the onions until soft and browned. Add the anchovy fillets and cook to a paste (approximately 5 minutes). Add the cream and milk and bring to the boil, then remove from the heat immediately. Mix with the potatoes, season well and put in a greased ovenproof dish. Cook in the preheated oven for 50 minutes–1 hour until nicely browned on top.

Tip
All the work involved in this dish is in the preparation of the potatoes, so if you can get someone to help here you can halve the preparation time.

Japaneasy Noodles
Serves 2
◔ **V**

Ingredients
160g packet yakisoba noodles
1 tablespoon (15ml) oil
1 bunch of spring onions, sliced
2 cloves garlic, crushed
2 teaspoons (10ml) minced chilli
1 teaspoon (5ml) minced ginger
¼ Savoy cabbage, finely shredded

Method
Cook the noodles in boiling water for 2 minutes, then drain. Meanwhile, heat the oil and fry the spring onions, garlic, chilli, ginger and cabbage. Add the noodles and sauce sachet to the other ingredients and stir. Serve hot or cold.

Hot 'n' Spicy Noodles
Serves 2
🕐 **V**

Ingredients
>   125g medium egg noodles
>   2 tablespoons (30ml) oil
>   ½ bunch of spring onions, sliced
>   2 cloves garlic, crushed
>   1 tablespoon (15ml) minced chilli
>   2 tablespoons (30ml) soy sauce

Method
Cook the noodles in boiling water for 4 minutes, then drain. Meanwhile, heat 1 tablespoon (15ml) of the oil and quickly stir-fry the spring onions, garlic and chilli. Add the drained noodles, soy sauce and the remaining oil, stir well and serve.

Noodle Salad
Serves 4
✳ ◔ **V**

Ingredients

For the salad
 225g medium egg noodles
 4 tomatoes, roughly chopped
 1 bunch of spring onions, chopped

For the dressing
 3 tablespoons (45ml) oil
 1 tablespoon (15ml) white wine vinegar
 1 tablespoon (15ml) soy sauce
 1 teaspoon (5ml) Dijon mustard
 1 teaspoon (5ml) honey or sugar

Method
Cook the noodles in boiling water for 4 minutes, then plunge them in cold water to stop them cooking and drain well. Mix the noodles with the tomatoes and spring onions. Put the dressing ingredients in a screw-top jar and shake well, then pour over the salad.

Curry-style Couscous
Serves 4
✳ ◷ **V Ve**

Ingredients
    250g couscous
    2 tablespoons raisins
    2 tablespoons toasted flaked almonds
    500ml vegetable stock, made with 1 stock cube and
       boiling water

Method
Place all the ingredients in a saucepan and bring to the boil.
Remove from the heat and allow to stand for 5 minutes until
the stock is absorbed. Stir before serving.

Tip
This is even nicer if you have some fresh coriander that you
can add to the finished dish.

Tabbouleh-style Salad
Serves 4
✳ **V Ve**

Ingredients
    125g bulgar wheat, soaked in water for 1 hour
    2 tomatoes, chopped
    1 green pepper, deseeded and diced
    ½ cucumber, diced
    1 bunch of coriander, chopped
    4 tablespoons (60ml) oil
    juice of 1 lemon
    salt and black pepper

Method
Squeeze out as much water as you can from the bulgar wheat. Mix the bulgar wheat with the tomatoes, green pepper, cucumber and coriander. Put the oil and lemon juice in a screw-top jar and shake well. Mix the dressing with the salad, season and serve.

Indian Pilau Rice
Serves 4
✳ ⏲

Ingredients
2 teaspoons (10ml) oil or butter
1 small onion, chopped
½ teaspoon whole coriander seeds
½ teaspoon whole cardamom pods
½ teaspoon whole cumin seeds
250g basmati rice, soaked
500ml chicken or vegetable stock, made with 1 stock
   cube and boiling water

Method
Heat the oil or butter and fry the onion until soft and just
starting to brown. Add the spices and stir-fry for 30
seconds–1 minute. This is just to get them to release their
flavours – be careful not to burn them. Add the rice, stir
quickly, then add the stock. Bring to the boil, cover tightly
and simmer for 10 minutes until the rice has absorbed the
stock. Take off the heat and allow to stand for 10 minutes
before stirring up the rice and serving.

Tip
If you forget to soak the rice, at least put it in a sieve and run
cold water through it before cooking.

Turkish Pilau Rice
Serves 4
✳ ◔ **V Ve**

Ingredients
>   1 tablespoon (15ml) oil
>   3 tablespoons pine nuts
>   1 onion, chopped
>   250g long-grain rice
>   6 whole cardamom seeds
>   700ml vegetable stock, made with 1 stock cube and
>   boiling water
>   salt and black pepper

Method
Heat the oil and fry the pine nuts until golden, then remove from the pan and use the oil to fry the onion. Add the rice and cardamom, stir, add the stock and season. Cook for about 15 minutes until the rice is cooked. Stir in the pine nuts before serving.

Chinese-style Rice
Serves 6–8
ⓒ **V**

Ingredients
400g basmati rice
2 tablespoons (30ml) oil
90g frozen peas
1 bunch of spring onions, chopped
1 tablespoon (15ml) soy sauce
2 eggs, beaten

Method
Cook the rice in boiling water until tender – about 15 minutes. Rinse in cold water and drain well. Heat the oil and stir-fry the rice, peas and spring onions for 2 minutes. Add the soy sauce and beaten egg and continue to stir-fry until the eggs set.

Nut and Apricot Dessert
Serves 2
✳ ◔ **V**

Ingredients
    100g Greek yogurt
    1 tablespoon toasted flaked almonds
    50g ready-to-eat apricots, sliced
    1 tablespoon sunflower seeds
    1 tablespoon (15ml) runny honey

Method
Place the yogurt in a dessert bowl and sprinkle with the almonds, apricots and sunflower seeds. Drizzle with the honey and serve immediately.

Tip
You can replace the almonds with toasted pine nuts: toast them on foil under the grill, watching carefully to ensure they don't burn.

Rhubarb Crumble
Serves 4
✳ **V**

Ingredients
- 500g rhubarb
- 1 tablespoon caster sugar
- juice of 1 large orange

For the crumble
- 75g butter
- 75g plain flour
- 75g + 1 tablespoon demerara sugar
- 75g porridge oats

Method
Preheat the oven to 200°C/400°F/Gas 6. Trim the ends off the rhubarb and cut into 3cm pieces. Place the rhubarb, caster sugar and orange juice in an ovenproof dish. Rub together the butter, flour and demerara sugar until you have a mixture resembling breadcrumbs. Stir in the porridge oats and spoon over the rhubarb. Sprinkle with the remaining tablespoon of demerara sugar. Cook, uncovered, in the preheated oven for 45–50 minutes. Leave to stand for 5–10 minutes before serving.

Tip
This is a favourite for a Sunday lunch dessert. Serve with cream, crème fraîche or custard. The crumble topping can be used to cover other seasonal fruit: soft fruit can be used as above but hard fruit should be gently stewed for 5–10 minutes before using.

Eton Mess
Serves 12
V

Ingredients
    750g strawberries, sliced
    2 tablespoons caster sugar
    12 small meringues, broken
    1 litre whipping cream, whipped until thick

Method
Mix together the strawberries and sugar and leave to chill for 1 hour to allow the strawberry juices to flow. When ready to make the pudding, mix all the ingredients together and pile into a huge bowl to serve.

Tip
Make this when strawberries are plentiful, not in the middle of winter when only imported expensive ones are available.

Cinnamon Rock Buns
Makes 6
✳ ☉ **V**

Ingredients
>   200g plain flour
>   1 teaspoon ground cinnamon
>   100g margarine
>   100g + 1 tablespoon demerara sugar
>   1 egg, beaten
>   2 tablespoons (30ml) milk

Method
Preheat the oven to 200°C/400°F/Gas 6. Rub together the flour, cinnamon, margarine and sugar until they resemble breadcrumbs. Stir in the egg and milk. Drop 6 spoonfuls of the mixture on to a baking tray and sprinkle with the remaining tablespoon of demerara sugar. Bake in the pre-heated oven for 20 minutes until golden brown. These buns are best served while still warm.

Tip
As the buns are made with plain flour they will not rise, but they smell divine while cooking and taste delicious.

Crispy-topped Flapjacks
Makes 12
V

Ingredients
>   150g melted butter
>   150g + 1 tablespoon demerara sugar
>   250g porridge oats

Method
Preheat the oven to 170°C/325°F/Gas 3. Combine the butter and demerara sugar. Add the oats and mix in really well. Put the mixture in a greased small roasting or baking tin (approximately 28 × 18cm) and level the surface with the back of a spoon. Sprinkle with the remaining tablespoon of demerara sugar and bake in the preheated oven for 30 minutes. Leave to stand in the tin for 10 minutes before turning out, then cut into squares or fingers to serve.

8 The Quick Snack

As students are often in a hurry when it comes to preparing meals, it is important to have a range of snacks that can be quickly put together. In fact, the diet of many students consists of snacks, snacks and more snacks! If you are not to fall into the trap of living off takeaways and processed foods (expensive and not particularly healthy), this is certainly a good chapter to get to grips with.

A big favourite with students is things on toast. However, as sometimes you may have to share one small grill with a large number of other students (often all trying to cook at the same time), it helps if you have a few other dishes that you can resort to if the queue for the grill looks too long for the time you have available.

Don't forget that if you can find time in the morning to prepare some sandwiches or filled rolls to take for your lunch, this is a good way of saving money. However, this only applies if you then actually eat them! If you end up going with friends to the canteen you will have paid for lunch twice.

Just a quick word of warning on health. If you find yourself living mainly on snacks, it becomes even more important to include plenty of fruit in your diet. This is not difficult as a piece of fruit is a ready packaged snack. There is only so long the human body can take being stuffed with chips, crisps, pastry, biscuits and chocolate before it rebels with spots, obesity, etc. The choice is yours . . .

Porridge
Serves 1

✳ ☉ **V**

The time it takes to cook the porridge will depend on the type of porridge oats you use – check the packet instructions.

Ingredients
> 50g porridge oats
> 250ml milk
> pinch of salt
> knob of butter (to serve)
> brown sugar (to serve)

Method
Put the oats, milk and salt in a saucepan and cook according to the packet instructions, stirring until you have a creamy consistency. Pour into a bowl, top with a knob of butter and a sprinkling of brown sugar.

Sandwiches

I've given you some of my favourite recipes for sandwiches here, but the main advantage of sandwiches is
their endless variety. You can ring the changes with the
many different types of bread or rolls now available.
Other options to consider are pitta bread, which is very
good stuffed, or chappatis, in which you can roll up
different fillings.

Suggestions for fillings:
cheese with mayo and corn
cheese and pickle (vary the type of pickle)
cheese with cucumber or tomatoes
soft cream cheese with chopped celery and mayo
hard-boiled egg with Marmite or chopped onion
hard-boiled egg with curry-flavoured mayo
chilli or bean spread with lettuce and/or cucumber
mashed beans with a little of your favourite salad
    dressing
peanut butter and jam (an American favourite)

Beansprouts with Hummus Sandwich
Serves 1
✳ ◷ **V**

Ingredients
 2 slices bread
 margarine to spread
 1 tablespoon (15ml) hummus
 2 tablespoons fresh beansprouts

Method
Spread bread with margarine. Spread 1 slice with hummus, top with beansprouts and then the remaining slice of bread. Serve within 30 minutes of making.

Brie and Grape Sandwich
Serves 1
✳ ◷ **V**

Ingredients
 2 slices bread
 margarine to spread
 25g Brie, sliced thinly
 3–4 grapes, halved

Method
Spread bread with margarine. Place cheese on one slice of bread, add grapes and top with the other slice of bread.

Peanut Butter and Banana Sandwich
Serves 1
✳ ◷ **V**

Ingredients
 2 slices bread
 margarine to spread
 2–3 teaspoons peanut butter
 1 small banana, mashed roughly

Method
Spread bread with margarine. Spread one slice with the peanut butter and then with the mashed banana. Top with the remaining slice of bread.

Salad Sandwich
Serves 1
✳ ◷ **V Ve**

Ingredients
> 2 slices bread, or 1 pitta bread, split
> 2 teaspoons (10ml) salad dressing
> 1 tomato, sliced
> few slices cucumber
> 1 lettuce leaf

Method
Spread both slices of bread with the salad dressing. Put the vegetables on one slice, then top with the other. If using pitta bread, stuff with vegetables and spoon in salad dressing.

Stuffed Pitta Bread
Serves 1
✳ ◷ **V**

Ingredients
> 1 pitta bread, split
> 50g feta cheese, sliced
> 1 tomato, sliced
> 1 teaspoon (5ml) oil
> 1 teaspoon (5ml) tomato purée

Method
Stuff the pitta bread with the feta cheese and tomato. Mix the oil and tomato purée and spoon into the pitta bread.

Toasted Cheese
Serves 1
⏲ **V**

This is probably the most popular remedy for those late night munchies.

Ingredients
> 2 slices bread
> 50g cheese
> 2 teaspoons soft margarine
> 1 teaspoon (5ml) French mustard

Method
Preheat the grill. Toast the bread on one side. Turn it over and toast the other side until it crisps but hasn't turned brown. Mash the cheese, margarine and mustard together and spread over the toast. Grill for about 2 minutes until bubbling and starting to brown.

Toasted cheese and tomato
As above, but add 2 teaspoons (10ml) tomato purée to the cheese mixture before toasting.

Toasted cheese and pickle
As in main recipe, but add 2 teaspoons (10ml) of your favourite pickle to the cheese mixture before toasting.

Fried Bread
Serves 1
✳ ⏲ **V Ve**

Ingredients
> 1 tablespoon (15ml) oil
> 1 slice bread, halved

Method
Heat the oil in a pan until very hot, add the bread and immediately turn it over. This ensures that both sides of the bread get coated with oil. Continue to cook, turning as necessary until both sides are crisp and brown. Serve with baked beans, fried eggs, tomatoes or mushrooms.

Cheese and Mango Toasties
Serves 1
🕐 **V**

This is my current version of a cheese and pickle toasted sandwich. You can vary this recipe by using different pickles or chutneys.

Ingredients
>   2 slices bread
>   25g cheese
>   1 teaspoon soft margarine
>   2 teaspoons (10ml) mango chutney

Method
Preheat the grill. Toast the bread slices on one side only. Meanwhile, mash together the cheese, margarine and mango chutney. Spread this mixture over one of the toasted slices of bread, top with the other slice, untoasted side up. Return to the grill and toast until brown. Turn the toastie over and brown the last untoasted side.

French Bread Pizza
Serves 1–2
🕐 **V**

Ingredients
>   1 French baguette, split
>   2 tablespoons (30ml) tomato purée
>   sprinkling of oregano
>   50g cheese, grated
>   2 tomatoes, sliced
>   black pepper

Method
Preheat the grill. Spread the tomato purée over the cut surfaces of the baguette. Sprinkle with the oregano and the cheese. Top with slices of tomato and season with black pepper. Grill for about 2 minutes until the cheese has melted and is beginning to bubble.

Carrot and Lentil Pâté
Serves 2–4
V

This is a very useful pâté which you can serve with French bread and salad as a lunch dish for 2 people or as a starter for 4.

Ingredients
> 100g split red lentils
> 100g carrots, grated
> 1 tablespoon (15ml) oil
> 1 onion, chopped
> 2 cloves garlic, crushed
> juice and grated rind of ½ lemon
> 1 teaspoon dried thyme
> 25g butter
> salt and pepper

Method
Cook the lentils in boiling water for 10 minutes, add the carrots, cover and simmer for a further 10 minutes. Heat the oil and fry the onion and garlic for 5 minutes, then add the lemon juice and rind and the thyme. Continue to cook for 3 minutes. Drain the lentil mixture thoroughly, beat in the butter. Mix everything together and season well. Chill for 1 hour before using.

Spicy Cheese and Nut Pâté
Serves 1
✳ ⏲ **V**

For the days when you want a change from a cheese sandwich or cheese and biscuits lunch, this is ideal. It makes a really delicious quick lunch with French bread or pitta bread.

Ingredients
> 21g cube of Danish Blue cheese
> 16g cube of Boursin with garlic and herbs
> 1 tablespoon soft margarine
> 15–25g Tobago Chilli flavoured roasted peanuts,
>   crushed or roughly chopped

Method
Mash together the cheeses and margarine. Stir in the peanuts and mix well.

Scrambled Eggs
Serves 1
✳ ◔ **V**

Ingredients
    2 eggs, beaten
    1 tablespoon (15ml) milk
    salt and pepper
    1 tablespoon soft margarine

Method
Beat the eggs and milk together. Season. Melt the margarine
in a small saucepan and add the egg mixture. Stir over a low
heat for 1–2 minutes until the eggs are set to your taste.
(Don't forget that they continue to cook a little after you take
them off the heat.)

Cheesy scrambled eggs
When you pour the egg and milk mixture into the pan add
25g grated cheese.

Savoury Scrambled Eggs
Serves 1
✳ ◔ **V**

Ingredients
    knob of butter
    3 spring onions, chopped
    2 eggs, beaten
    1 tablespoon (15ml) milk
    ¼ teaspoon Marmite
    pepper

Method
Melt the butter in a small frying pan and cook the onions for
1 minute. Beat together the eggs, milk and Marmite. Pour
into the pan and cook, stirring, for 1–2 minutes until the egg
has set to a creamy consistency. Serve with buttered toast.

Divine Summer Soup
Serves 2
✳ ◔ **V Ve**

A really quick and easy soup which I absolutely love.

Ingredients
 1 tablespoon (15ml) oil
 200g new potatoes, skinned and diced
 200g red and orange peppers, sliced
 200g courgettes, halved and sliced
 pinch of dried oregano
 500ml vegetable stock
 salt and pepper

Method
Start by heating the oil and frying the potatoes for about 5 minutes until starting to brown. Add the peppers and courgettes and cook for a few minutes until starting to soften. Add the other ingredients, raise the heat until just starting to boil and then cover and simmer for 10 minutes.

Egg and Vegetable Hash
Serves 2
✳ ◷ **V**

This uses the same vegetables as the Divine Summer Soup (opposite), so if cooking for one you could cook this up until the time when you add the eggs and then keep half of the cooked vegetables to make soup with the next day or to have as your evening meal with some chunky bread and some cheese. Many snacks can be turned into full meals by adding bread, cheese, salad or vegetables to them.

Ingredients
> 1 tablespoon (15ml) oil
> 200g new potatoes, skinned and diced
> 200g red and orange peppers, sliced
> 200g courgettes, halved and sliced
> pinch of dried oregano
> 4–6 eggs (depending on appetite)
> salt and pepper

Method
Heat the oil and fry the potatoes for 5 minutes and then add the other vegetables. Continue to fry for 5 minutes, add the oregano and then carefully break the eggs over the vegetables. Cover and cook for 3–5 minutes until the whites are cooked but the yolks still have a 'wobble'. Season and divide between 2 plates to serve. Great with some bread and tomato ketchup or brown sauce.

Huevos Rancheros
Serves 1
🕐 **V**

This is very quick and easy to make and always popular for breakfast or lunch. If you have some coriander (either fresh or dried) you could add a little for a really authentic taste. You could also serve it with some oven chips for a tasty supper.

Ingredients
    230g can chopped tomatoes
    chilli sauce *or* powder to taste
    oil for frying
    2 eggs

Method
In a small saucepan heat the tomatoes gently for 10 minutes, until reduced to a sauce. Add chilli to taste. Cover the bottom of a frying pan with oil and heat. Gently break in the eggs. Baste with oil until the yolks become opaque. Spoon the sauce on to a plate and arrange the eggs on top.

Egg, Tomato and Mushroom Fry-up
Serves 1
✳ 🕐 **V**

Ingredients
    knob of butter
    100g button mushrooms
    1 tomato, quartered lengthways
    1 tablespoon (15ml) oil
    1 egg
    salt and pepper

Method
Melt the butter and cook the mushrooms and tomato for 3–4 minutes. Push to one side of the pan, add the oil and, when it is hot, break the egg carefully into the pan. Season with salt and pepper. Baste the egg with the hot oil until cooked, then serve immediately.

Boiled Eggs and Marmite Soldiers
Serves 1
🕐 **V**

There are some who think that recipes for boiled eggs or for baked beans on toast are unnecessary. Perhaps they are unaware of the novice cooks who have tried to cook beans without first removing them from the tin or who have tried to fry onions, whole and without first peeling them! It's difficult to decide just how much detail to go into but I like to think that if you have made it to uni in the first place, you must have some intelligence and common sense.

Ingredients
>   2 eggs
>   2 slices bread
>   margarine
>   Marmite

Method
Boil some water in a saucepan. Add the eggs carefully and boil for 4 minutes. Toast the bread and spread with margarine and Marmite. Cut each slice into 5 lengths and serve with the boiled eggs.

Baked Beans on Toast
Serves 1
🕐 **V**

Ingredients
>   200–400g can baked beans (depending on appetite!)
>   2 slices bread
>   margarine

Method
Toast the bread while warming the beans in a small saucepan. Spread the toast with margarine and top with beans. Grated cheese or chilli sauce can be added to vary this feast.

The Alternative Beans on Toast
Serves 1
🕒 **V**

Ingredients
> ½ 430g can chilli beans
> 2 petits pains rolls or 20cm French baguette
> 25g cheese, grated

Method
Preheat the grill. In a small saucepan heat the beans. Do not boil. Split open the rolls or baguette and place on a heat-proof tray. Pile the beans on to the bread, sprinkle with the cheese and grill for 2–3 minutes, until the cheese has melted and is bubbling.

Fried Potatoes
Serves 1
✳ 🕒 **V Ve**

Ingredients
> 75g potatoes, peeled and cubed
> 1 tablespoon (15ml) oil
> salt and pepper

Method
Mix the potatoes and oil in a bowl and season well. Heat a frying pan until hot, add the oil-covered potatoes and fry until brown on all sides. This should take about 6–10 minutes, depending on the size of your potato cubes.

9 Cooking for One

In your first term (or maybe even your first year) at uni, the chances are that whether you live in hall, a student flat or a bedsit, the cooking you do will usually be for one. Later on you will probably find friends that you can share the cooking with at least some of the time.

It's a well-known fact that many people, faced with cooking for one, just don't bother. But . . . it is a good way of saving money and it's better for your diet than continually living off processed food. (Look at the ingredients next time you buy a ready made meal – do you really want all those additives?) There are many meals for one that can be cooked in minutes and are really very easy to prepare. At the beginning of term being busy in the kitchen is a great way of meeting people and making new friends. (Many years later, two of my best friends are people I shared a kitchen with that first year.) So even if you haven't had a great deal to do with the kitchen up until now, this is the time to get to grips with its pleasures!

Mexican Bean Soup
Serves 1
✳ ⏱ **V**

This is a really easy soup to make and is a great supper dish.
You can also make it with beans in chilli sauce. A small
portion would be a delicious starter for a Mexican meal.

Ingredients
>   1 tablespoon (15ml) oil
>   1 small onion, chopped
>   1 small green pepper, diced
>   225g can beans in spicy sauce
>   225g can chopped tomatoes
>   tortilla chips (to serve)
>   grated cheese (to serve)

Method
Heat the oil in a small saucepan and fry the onion and
pepper for 10 minutes until soft and starting to brown. Add
the beans and tomatoes and stir well. Simmer gently for
10–15 minutes. Serve topped with tortilla chips and grated
cheese.

Provençale Salad
Serves 1
☉ **V**

You can of course use ordinary tomatoes for this recipe, but I prefer 'beef' tomatoes (the big slicing variety). You could also use just one type of pepper instead of the two I have – but using two adds to the colourfulness of this dish.

Ingredients
 1 egg
 ½ red pepper
 ½ green pepper
 1 courgette, grated
 1 'beef' tomato, sliced
 few slices red onion
 25g black pitted olives, halved

For the dressing
 1 tablespoon (15ml) tomato purée
 1 tablespoon (15ml) oil
 1 teaspoon (5ml) wine vinegar
 1 clove garlic, crushed
 salt and pepper

Method
Boil the egg for 10 minutes and then leave to cool. Preheat the grill. Cut each pepper in half, grill, skin side up, until the skin blackens, then cut into strips. Shell the boiled egg and cut into wedges. Arrange the salad ingredients on a plate. Mix together all the dressing ingredients and drizzle over the salad.

Spicy Chinese Salad
Serves 1
✳ ◷ **V Ve**

Ingredients
>100g fresh beansprouts
>2 Chinese cabbage leaves, chopped
>100g can sweetcorn
>1/2 red pepper, diced
>2 spring onions, chopped
>2 celery sticks, chopped

For the dressing
>1 tablespoon (15ml) tomato purée *or* ketchup
>1 tablespoon (15ml) wine vinegar
>1 tablespoon (15ml) soy sauce
>2 tablespoons (30 ml) orange juice
>1/2 teaspoon (2.5ml) ginger purée

Method
Mix all the salad ingredients together. Now mix all the dressing ingredients together and pour over the salad.

Hula Hoops Salad
Serves 1
✳ ◷ **V**

This is a really crunchy salad that makes an ideal lunch dish – but prepare it at the last minute or the Hula Hoops will go soft.

Ingredients
>1/2 198g can sweetcorn, drained
>2 celery sticks, sliced
>2 tomatoes, sliced *or* 6 cherry tomatoes
>30g packet original Hula Hoops

For the dressing
>2 tablespoons (30ml) cheese and chive spread
>1 tablespoon (15ml) natural yogurt

Method
Put all the salad ingredients in a serving bowl. Beat together the cheese and chive spread and the yogurt until smooth. Dress the salad and serve immediately.

Carrot Salad
Serves 1
✳ ☻ **V**

An easy side salad that goes with most dishes – I particularly like it with curries.

Ingredients
> 100g carrots, grated

For the dressing
> 1 tablespoon (15ml) oil
> 1 tablespoon (15ml) orange juice
> 1 teaspoon (5ml) whole-grain mustard
> 1 teaspoon (5ml) white wine vinegar

Method
Mix all the dressing ingredients together and pour over the grated carrot. Serve.

Tomato, Cheese and Courgette Salad
Serves 1
✳ ☻ **V**

Ingredients
> 2 large tomatoes
> 1 courgette, grated
> 50g cheese, sliced

For the dressing
> 1 tablespoon (15ml) oil
> 1 tablespoon (15ml) tomato ketchup
> salt and pepper

Method
Dice one tomato, mix with the courgette and place on a serving plate. Slice the other tomato. Cover the courgette and diced tomato mixture with slices of cheese and tomato. Mix together the dressing ingredients and spoon over the salad. Serve.

Mexican Salad
Serves 1
✳ ⊙ **V Ve**

Ingredients
    1 avocado, peeled, stoned and halved
    pinch of coriander
    2 tomatoes, sliced
    ½ 200g can red kidney beans, drained
    few slices of red onion
    1 tablespoon (15ml) tomato purée
    1 tablespoon (15ml) oil
    1 teaspoon (5ml) wine vinegar
    few drops of chilli sauce

Method
Thinly slice one half of the avocado on to a plate. Roughly mash the other half and mix with the coriander. Place this on your plate, and beside it put the sliced tomatoes. Now mix the remaining ingredients and scatter over the avocado and tomatoes. Serve immediately.

Veggie Varsity Pie
Serves 1
⊙ **V**

When *Grub on a Grant* was first published my Varsity Pie was one of the first recipes to prove popular. Therefore I felt I really ought to include a veggie version in this book.

Ingredients
    125g can condensed mushroom soup
    100g can sweetcorn
    100g can beans
    2 slices wholemeal bread, buttered
    25g cheese, grated

Method
Preheat the oven to 190°C/375°F/Gas 5. Mix together the soup, sweetcorn and beans and put into a small casserole dish. Halve the bread and place, buttered side up, on top of the mixture. Sprinkle with the grated cheese and bake in the preheated oven for 25 minutes.

Undone Pie

Serves 1
🕐 **V**

Ingredients

125g can condensed vegetable soup
200g can baked beans
1 tablespoon (15ml) tomato purée
1 tomato, sliced
2 thick slices French bread, buttered
50g cheese, grated

Method

Preheat the oven to 180°C/350°F/Gas 4. Mix the soup, beans and tomato purée together. Arrange the tomato slices in the bottom of a small ovenproof dish. Cover with the soup mixture. Cut the bread slices in half and use to top the dish. Sprinkle with the cheese and bake in the preheated oven for 25 minutes.

Butter Bean Bake

Serves 1
🕐 **V**

Ingredients

200g can butter beans
125g can condensed mushroom soup
1–2 slices wholemeal bread, buttered
25g cheese, grated

Method

Preheat the oven to 180°C/350°F/Gas 4. Put the beans and soup into a small casserole dish. Cut the bread slices in half and arrange them, buttered side up, over the top. Sprinkle with the cheese and bake in the preheated oven for 25 minutes.

Vegetarian Bolognese Bake
Serves 1
✳ **V**

Ingredients
> 1 portion Vegetarian Bolognese Sauce (page 215)
> 1 tomato, thinly sliced
> 25g cheese, grated
> 200g baked potato, sliced
> melted butter *or* margarine

Method
Preheat the oven to 200°C/400°F/Gas 6. Place the bolognese sauce in a casserole dish and cover with the sliced tomato and cheese. Arrange the potato slices on top and brush with melted butter or margarine. Bake in the preheated oven for 30 minutes.

Curried Bean Crumble
Serves 1
🕐 **V**

Ingredients
> 1 tablespoon (15ml) oil
> 1 onion, diced
> ½ green pepper, diced
> 200g can curried beans
> 2 slices wholemeal bread, crumbed
> 25g cheese, grated

Method
Preheat the grill. Heat the oil and fry the onion and pepper until soft. Add the beans and heat gently. Transfer to a flameproof dish. Mix together the breadcrumbs and cheese and sprinkle over the vegetables. Grill until the cheese melts. Serve immediately.

Bean Bangers
Serves 1
⏲ **V Ve**

Ingredients
>   200g can barbecue beans, drained, reserving the sauce
>   2 slices bread, crusts removed and crumbed
>   dried wholemeal crumbs for coating
>   oil for frying

Method
Mash the beans and mix with the fresh breadcrumbs. Divide
the mixture into four, and carefully shape into four small
sausages (fat and thick rather than long and thin). Put plenty of
dried crumbs on a plate. Roll the sausages in the crumbs,
patting into all sides. Heat enough oil in a small frying pan to
just cover the bottom and fry the bangers for 3–4 minutes until
brown all over. Meanwhile, heat the reserved barbecue sauce
gently in a small pan; serve with the bean bangers.

Baked Cheese Sandwich
Serves 1
⏲ **V**

Ingredients
>   2 slices bread, buttered
>   25 50g cheese, grated
>   dab of Marmite
>   1 teaspoon (5ml) tomato purée
>   125ml milk
>   1 egg, beaten
>   salt and pepper

Method
Preheat the oven to 180°C/350°F/Gas 4. Pile the cheese on
to one slice of buttered bread and spread the other with the
Marmite and tomato purée. Sandwich together and cut into 4
triangles. Place in a small ovenproof dish. Beat together the
milk and egg. Season. Pour over the sandwich, pushing the
bread into the milk and egg mixture to ensure it gets well
coated. Bake in the preheated oven for 25–35 minutes until
the top is browned.

Cheese and Tomato Vegetables
Serves 1
✳ ☾ **V**

This is a really useful recipe to master as it is very easy and cheap.

Ingredients
> 2 tablespoons (30ml) oil
> 1 onion, chopped
> 2 cloves garlic, chopped
> 100g mushrooms, sliced
> 1 small courgette, quartered and sliced
> 3 tomatoes, quartered and sliced
> 2 tablespoons (30ml) tomato purée
> 25g cheese, grated
> salt and pepper

Method
Heat the oil and fry the onion, garlic, mushrooms and courgette for 10 minutes. Add the tomatoes and tomato purée and cook for a further 5 minutes. Stir in the cheese and season. Serve with pasta or as a topping for baked potatoes.

Cheese and Potato Cakes
Serves 1
V

Ingredients
> 200g potatoes, cut into chunks
> 1 egg, beaten
> 50g cheese, grated
> 2 spring onions, chopped
> salt and pepper
> dried wholemeal crumbs *or* wholemeal flour for coating
> oil for frying

Method
Cook the potatoes in boiling water until tender (about 15 minutes). Drain, mash and mix with the egg, cheese and onions. Season. As soon as the mixture is cool enough to handle, divide into two portions and gently shape into two cakes. Coat with crumbs or flour and leave to stand for 30 minutes. Heat enough oil to coat the bottom of a frying pan and cook the cakes for 2 minutes on each side until brown.

Quick Fried Cheese 'n' Tomato Pizza
Serves 1–2
🕐 **V**

Ingredients
150g self-raising flour
pinch of salt
1 tablespoon (15ml) oil
oil to grease frying pan
2 tablespoons (30ml) tomato purée
sprinkling of oregano
1 tomato, sliced
25g cheese, grated

Method
Preheat the grill. Mix the flour, salt and oil together with enough warm water (about 6 tablespoons/90ml) to make a dough. Knead for a couple of minutes until the dough is pliable. Grease a large frying pan lightly with oil. Press out the dough to fill the pan. Fry for 4 minutes then turn the dough and fry other side. Spread with the tomato purée, sprinkle the oregano over it, and top with the tomato slices and cheese. Grill until the cheese melts and is bubbling.

Quick fried cheese 'n' mushroom pizza
Substitute 100g mushrooms for the tomato. Gently fry the mushrooms in some butter before starting to make the pizza, then cook as above.

Pasta and Mushrooms with Hummus Sauce
Serves 1
🕐 **V**

Ingredients
> 75g pasta
> oil for frying
> 1 small onion, chopped
> 1 clove garlic, chopped
> 100g mushrooms, sliced
> 100g hummus
> 1 tablespoon (15ml) milk
> salt and pepper

Method
Add your chosen pasta to a saucepan of boiling water. While it's cooking (about 10–12 minutes) make the sauce. Heat the oil and fry the onion and garlic until they start to colour. Add the mushrooms and continue to cook until soft. Stir in the hummus and milk. Cover and simmer gently for a few minutes. When the pasta is cooked, drain. Season the sauce and serve with the pasta.

Avocado and Banana with Pasta
Serves 1
✳ 🕐 **V**

This is a particular favourite of mine. It is full of calories, but very easy to make and very tasty.

Ingredients
> 75g pasta
> 1 tablespoon soft margarine
> 1 tablespoon smooth peanut butter
> 1 ripe avocado, peeled, stoned and chopped
> 1 ripe banana, chopped
> black pepper

Method
Cook the pasta in boiling water until 'al dente' (cooked but still retaining some 'bite'). Beat together the margarine and peanut butter. When the pasta is cooked, drain and add the other ingredients. Season with black pepper. Return to the heat briefly to warm ingredients through. Serve immediately.

Tomato Provençale and Spaghetti
Serves 1
⊕ **V Ve**

Ingredients
- 75g spaghetti
- 200g can tomatoes
- 2 tablespoons (30ml) oil
- 2 mushrooms, sliced
- 1 clove garlic, crushed
- pinch of mixed herbs

Method
Cook the spaghetti in boiling water. Drain the tomatoes, reserving half of the juice and chop roughly. Heat the oil and fry the tomatoes, mushrooms and garlic. Add the reserved juice and herbs and simmer until the spaghetti is ready. Then drain the spaghetti, pour the sauce over it and serve.

Mushnut Sauce *(for pasta)*
Serves 1
✳ ⊕ **V**

Ingredients
- 2 tablespoons (30ml) oil
- 1 onion, chopped
- 1 clove garlic, crushed
- 100g mushrooms, sliced
- 1 teaspoon (5ml) tomato purée
- 1 tablespoon roasted chopped hazelnuts
- 2 tablespoons (30ml) crème fraîche
- salt and pepper

Method
Heat the oil and fry the onion, garlic and mushrooms until soft. Add the tomato purée, hazelnuts and crème fraîche, plus 3 tablespoons (45ml) water. Stir until it has heated through, season and serve with pasta.

Green Lentil Sauce *(for pasta)*
Serves 1
✳ ◷ **V**

Ingredients
    50g green lentils
    2 tablespoons (30ml) creamy pesto

Method
Cook the green lentils in boiling water for 10 minutes, then simmer for a further 20. Drain, mix in the pesto and serve with pasta.

Red Lentil Sauce *(for pasta)*
Serves 1
✳ ◷ **V**

Ingredients
    25g split red lentils
    1 teaspoon (5ml) Marmite
    1 tablespoon (15ml) tomato ketchup

Method
Boil the lentils in 250ml water for 15 minutes, until cooked and reduced to a runny sauce. Add the Marmite and ketchup, stir well and use to top pasta or a baked potato.

Vegetarian Bolognese Sauce
Makes 2 portions
✳ ☉ **V Ve**

Use half this recipe as a topping for spaghetti and keep half to use the next day in Vegetarian Bolognese Bake (page 208). It can also be used as a filling for baked potatoes.

Ingredients
>   1 tablespoon (15ml) oil
>   1 onion, chopped
>   2 cloves garlic, crushed
>   1 large carrot, finely diced
>   100g mushrooms, chopped
>   1 tablespoon (15ml) tomato purée
>   250g can chopped tomatoes
>   50g bulgar wheat
>   1 tablespoon (15ml) soy sauce

Method
Heat the oil and fry the onion, garlic and carrot for 5 minutes. Add the mushrooms and continue to cook for 5 minutes. Add the remaining ingredients, pour in 200ml water and bring to the boil. Cover and simmer for 15 minutes.

Carrot and Courgette Stir-fry
Serves 1
✳ ☉ **V Ve**

Ingredients
>   1 teaspoon (5ml) oil
>   1 carrot, cut into matchsticks
>   1 courgette, cut into matchsticks
>   225g can pineapple pieces, drained but reserve
>   1 tablespoon (15ml) pineapple juice
>   1 tablespoon (15ml) tomato ketchup
>   1 tablespoon (15ml) soy sauce
>   1 teaspoon (5ml) wine vinegar
>   ½ teaspoon cornflour

Method
Heat the oil and stir-fry the carrot and courgette for 3–4 minutes. Add the pineapple pieces. Mix together the other ingredients, add to the pan and simmer for 2–3 minutes until heated through.

Veggies in Cheese Sauce
Serves 1
🕐 **V**

This is a useful recipe for a quick supper. Sometimes I add a little cream to the sauce and just serve it with crusty French bread.

Ingredients
>   150g cauliflower florets
>   100g carrots, sliced
>   50g frozen peas
>   1 tablespoon margarine
>   1 tablespoon plain flour
>   1 teaspoon (5ml) French mustard
>   125ml milk
>   50g cheese, grated

Method
Cook the cauliflower and carrots in boiling water for 7 minutes. Add the peas and continue to cook for 3 minutes. Drain. Meanwhile, make the sauce. Melt the margarine in a small pan, remove from the heat, stir in the flour and mustard, and gradually add just enough milk to make a smooth sauce. Return to the heat and as the sauce thickens add the remaining milk. Cook for 1 minute, then add the cheese. Mix with the cooked vegetables. Serve with rice or pasta.

Stir-fried Vegetables with Noodles
Serves 1–2
🕐 **V Ve**

Ingredients
>   85g Doll instant noodles with wonton-flavoured soup base
>   1 tablespoon (15ml) oil
>   1 carrot, thinly sliced
>   2 celery sticks, thinly sliced
>   50g mushrooms, thinly sliced
>   3 spring onions, thinly sliced
>   ½ 190g can sweetcorn
>   ½ 350g can beansprouts
>   1 tablespoon (15ml) soy sauce
>   sprinkling of peanuts or sesame seeds

Method
Using 375ml boiling water, cook the noodles as directed on packet. Heat the oil and stir-fry the carrot, celery and mushrooms for 2 minutes. Add the spring onions, sweetcorn and beansprouts and continue stir-frying for another 2 minutes. Sieve the noodles and add to the pan. Cook for 2 minutes. Stir in the soy sauce and peanuts or sesame seeds and serve.

10-minute Curry
Serves 1
✳ ☉ **V**

Well, I can cook this in 10 minutes! It depends on how quick you are at chopping up vegetables. Heat the oil while you prepare your veg, unless you are particularly slow – then you may risk burning the oil before you're ready to start.

Ingredients
    1 tablespoon (15ml) oil
    1 onion, chopped
    1 clove garlic, crushed
    100g mushrooms, sliced
    2 teaspoons (10ml) balti paste
    1 teaspoon (5ml) tomato purée
    200g can curried baked beans
    1 tablespoon (15ml) mango chutney (optional)
    1 tablespoon (15ml) crème fraîche (optional)

Method
Heat the oil and fry the onion, garlic and mushrooms for 5 minutes. Stir in the balti paste and the tomato purée and cook for 1 minute. Pour in 150ml boiling water and simmer for 2 minutes. Add the beans, and the chutney and crème fraîche (if using), and heat through. Serve.

Chick Pea Curry
Serves 1
✳ ⊙ **V Ve**

You can use fresh chopped mint or mint sauce with this – but don't use dried mint.

Ingredients
    1 tablespoon (15ml) oil
    1 onion, chopped
    1 clove garlic, crushed
    1 tablespoon (15ml) balti paste
    200g can chopped tomatoes
    400g can chick peas, drained
    1 tablespoon mint, chopped *or* mint sauce

Method
Heat the oil and fry the onion and garlic until soft. Stir in the balti paste and cook for 1 minute. Add the tomatoes and chick peas and simmer for 10 minutes. Add the mint just before serving.

Fruity Curry Sauce
Serves 1
✳ ◷ **V**

This is a very easy sauce, that you will probably use time and time again.

Ingredients
  1 tablespoon (15ml) oil
  1 onion, diced
  2 tablespoons (30ml) balti paste
  1 tablespoon (15ml) tomato purée
  1 tablespoon (15ml) mango chutney
  2 tablespoons (30ml) crème fraîche
  1–2 tablespoons chopped fresh coriander

Method
Heat the oil and fry the onion until soft. Stir in the balti paste and tomato purée and cook for 2 minutes. Pour in 150ml boiling water and simmer for 5 minutes. Now add the rest of the ingredients and the sauce is ready to serve mixed with cooked vegetables, beans or hard-boiled eggs.

Lentil and Coconut Dhal
Serves 1
V

Ingredients
  2 tablespoons desiccated coconut
  2 tablespoons (30ml) oil
  1 onion, chopped
  1 clove garlic, crushed
  2 teaspoons (10ml) balti paste
  50g split red lentils
  knob of butter

Method
Put the coconut into a bowl and just cover with boiling water. Leave to stand for 30 minutes. Heat the oil and fry the onion and garlic for 5 minutes. Add the balti paste and stir-fry for 2 minutes. Add the lentils and 150ml boiling water and simmer for 20 minutes, adding more water if necessary. Finally, add the coconut and stir in a knob of butter. Serve immediately with rice.

Chinese Rice with Omelette
Serves 1
🕐 **V**

Ingredients
>   100g basmati rice
>   250ml vegetable stock
>   25g butter
>   50g mushrooms, sliced
>   1 tablespoon frozen peas
>   3 spring onions, chopped
>   1 egg, beaten
>   1 tablespoon (15ml) milk
>   salt and pepper
>   1 tablespoon (15ml) soy sauce

Method
Put the rice and stock in a saucepan and bring to the boil.
Cover and simmer for 10–12 minutes until all the stock has
been absorbed. Meanwhile, melt half the butter and stir-fry
the mushrooms, peas and spring onions for 3–4 minutes. Set
aside. Beat together the egg and milk and season. Melt the
rest of the butter in a small frying pan and pour in the egg
mixture. Tilt the pan so that the egg covers the bottom of the
pan. Draw the cooked egg into the middle of the pan,
allowing the uncooked mixture to run underneath and set.
When the egg has set, slide on to a plate, roll it up and cut
into little egg rolls. When the rice is cooked add the soy
sauce and mix in the stir-fried vegetables. Put in a bowl and
serve with the egg rolls on top.

Broad Bean, Onion and Coriander Pilau
Serves 1
🕐 **V Ve**

You really need fresh coriander for this dish. If you cannot get it, substitute fresh mint or mint sauce.

Ingredients
- 75g basmati rice
- 2 tablespoons (30ml) oil
- 2 onions, sliced
- 2 tablespoons fresh coriander, chopped
- 300g can broad beans, drained

Method
Cook the basmati rice in boiling water. Meanwhile, heat the oil and fry the onions until quite brown. When the rice is cooked, mix in the coriander, the beans and half the fried onion. Arrange the remainder of the onions on top and serve.

Quick Chilli 'n' Tomato Sauce
Serves 1
✳ 🕐 **V Ve**

Ingredients
- 1 tablespoon (15ml) chilli relish
- 1 tablespoon (15ml) tomato purée
- 1 tablespoon (15ml) boiling water

Method
Mix all the ingredients together and use as a sauce for savoury dishes.

Lentil and Bulgar Kedgeree
Serves 1
V Ve
Ingredients
>   25g green lentils
>   50g bulgar wheat
>   1 teaspoon (5ml) oil
>   1 onion, sliced
>   1 carrot, cut into matchsticks
>   2 teaspoons (10ml) balti paste

Method
Boil the green lentils in plenty of water for 10 minutes. Then reduce the heat and simmer for 10 minutes. Add the bulgar and continue to cook for 15 minutes. Meanwhile, heat the oil and fry the onion and carrot until they start to colour. Add the balti paste and cook for 1 minute, stirring. Pour in 100ml boiling water, stir well and simmer for 5 minutes. When the lentils and bulgar are cooked, drain and mix with curried vegetables.

Cheese Omelette
Serves 1
   ✳ ☉ **V**
Ingredients
>   2–3 eggs, beaten
>   1 tablespoon (15ml) milk *or* cold water
>   50g cheese, grated
>   salt and pepper
>   knob of butter

Method
Beat the eggs and milk or water. Add half the cheese and season. Melt the butter in a small frying pan. Pour in the egg mixture and swirl over the bottom of the pan. Draw the cooked egg into the middle, allowing the uncooked mixture to run underneath and set. When the egg has set, sprinkle the remaining cheese on top. Slide the omelette on to your plate, folding one half of the omelette over the other.

Mushroom omelette
Gently fry 100g sliced button mushrooms in some butter until soft. Keep to one side while you cook the omelette as above but omitting the cheese. Add the mushrooms to the cooked omelette before sliding on to your plate.

10 Cooking with Friends

This is where the fun starts. We had some great laughs while busily preparing meals. It's when people come together at the end of the day that you get to hear all the latest gossip, find out what's going on in the world, and learn what's planned for the evening, weekend – and get the reports on what happened last night . . .

If you have nothing particular planned for an evening, why not invite a friend or two over for a meal? A leisurely meal followed by a trip to the bar was one of our favourite ways of spending the evening (winning hands down every time over *really* getting to grips with that essay).

If you are living in a communal household, although it is not usual to cook for everyone every night, it is common to have a kitty for some items, such as milk, bread, tea and coffee. (It is also common to have arguments about who's paid, who's finished the milk and so on!) If someone offers to cook one evening, the cost of the meal is divided between those taking part.

If you are living in a shared house, hopefully you will not have the problem of people nicking your foodstuffs (or at least they should be able to provide a plausible

excuse as to why they did so!). You should therefore be able to make more use of fresh vegetables in your cooking. You will soon find that an additional bonus is that it works out cheaper per head to cook in quantity.

Bulgar Wheat Salad with Peanut Sauce
Serves 2–4
◔ **V**

Ingredients
> 100g bulgar wheat
> knob of butter
> 100g mushrooms, sliced
> 1 avocado, peeled, stoned and diced
> 3 tomatoes, skinned

For the peanut sauce
> 150g crunchy peanut butter
> 2 tablespoons (30ml) soy sauce
> 1 tablespoon soft brown sugar
> 1 tablespoon (15ml) lemon juice

Method
Cook the bulgar wheat in boiling water for 10–15 minutes until tender; drain well. Melt the butter in a pan and cook the mushrooms for 3–4 minutes; mix with the other salad ingredients. Gently heat the peanut butter, soy sauce, sugar, lemon juice and 100 ml water and beat well to form a sauce. Pour over the salad.

Curried Bean and Fruit Salad
Serves 4
✳ ◔ **V Ve**

Ingredients
> 1 tablespoon (15ml) oil
> 1 onion, chopped
> 1 clove garlic, crushed
> 1 tablespoon (15ml) curry paste
> 225g can pineapple pieces in pineapple juice
> 1 banana, sliced
> 400g can chick peas, drained
> 400g can red kidney beans, drained

Method
Heat the oil and fry the onion and garlic for 7 minutes until soft and starting to colour. Add the curry paste and the contents of the can of pineapple, including the juice. Simmer gently for 3 minutes. Add the remaining ingredients and stir well. Cool before serving.

Pasta Salad
Serves 4–5
⏲ **V Ve**

Ingredients
    250g pasta bows
    1 tablespoon (15ml) oil
    1 onion, chopped
    1 red pepper, diced
    1 clove garlic, crushed
    1 courgette, diced
    100g mushrooms, sliced

For the dressing
    1 clove garlic, crushed
    1 teaspoon salt
    $\frac{1}{2}$ teaspoon mustard powder
    1 tablespoon (15ml) lemon juice
    2 tablespoons (30ml) oil

Method
Cook the pasta in boiling water until 'al dente', then drain. Meanwhile, heat the oil and fry the onion, pepper and garlic for 5 minutes, add the courgette and mushrooms and cook for a further 5 minutes. Add to the pasta. Mix all the dressing ingredients together, pour over the pasta and vegetables and stir well.

Rice Salad
Serves 4
✳ ◷ **V**

This is a great, really fresh tasting salad. Prepare it just before you are ready to eat as it tastes much better freshly dressed.

Ingredients
> 200g brown rice, cooked and cooled
> 198g can sweetcorn, drained
> 100g frozen peas, cooked and cooled
> 2–3 tomatoes, skinned and chopped

For the dressing
> 1 clove garlic, crushed
> 1 teaspoon salt
> 1/2 teaspoon mustard powder
> 1 tablespoon (15ml) lemon juice
> 2 tablespoons (30ml) low-fat natural yogurt

Method
Combine all the salad ingredients. Mix all the dressing ingredients. Pour the dressing over the salad, stir well and serve immediately.

Coleslaw with Apple
Serves 3–4
✳ ◷ **V**

Ingredients
> 200g white cabbage, thinly sliced
> 100g carrot, grated
> 100g apple, grated
> 2 tablespoons (30ml) mayonnaise
> 1 dessertspoon (10ml) white wine vinegar
> salt and pepper

Method
Put the cabbage, carrot and apple in a bowl. Mix together the mayonnaise and vinegar and pour into the bowl. Stir thoroughly. Season.

Shortcrust Pastry
Makes 300g
🕐 **V**

Although you can buy pastry either frozen or chilled, here are some recipes that you may want to try. Don't worry if you have trouble rolling out your pastry – you can press it into your dish.

Ingredients
> 200g flour
> pinch of salt
> 125g butter
> cold water

Method
Put the flour, salt and butter into a bowl. Rub the mixture between your fingertips until it resembles fine breadcrumbs. Add a few tablespoons of water – only as much as you need to form a dough. Wrap the dough in clingfilm and rest it in the fridge for 20 minutes before using. Roll out on a floured surface with a rolling pin, handling the dough as little as possible.

Cheese pastry
Add 75g grated cheese, a pinch of dried mustard powder and an egg yolk to the 'breadcrumb' mixture.

Nutty pastry
Add 50g roasted chopped hazelnuts and an egg yolk to the 'breadcrumb' mixture.

Baking 'blind'
This helps to produce a crispy pastry shell for quiches. Preheat the oven to 190°C/375°F/Gas 5. Line a 20cm flan tin with the pastry, then prick the base of the pastry all over with a fork. Put some greaseproof paper in the bottom and weigh down with some coins. Bake in the preheated oven for 15 minutes. Remove paper and coins before using.

Broccoli, Cheese and Tomato Quiche
Serves 3–4
V

To skin tomatoes, put them in a bowl, cover with boiling water and leave until the skin can be easily peeled away. Be careful when taking the tomatoes out as the water will still be very hot!
Ingredients
> 300g Cheese Pastry (page 230)
> 150g broccoli florets, cooked
> 2 plum tomatoes, skinned and cut into wedges
> 75g cheese, grated
> 2 eggs, beaten
> 125ml carton single cream
> salt and pepper
> few chopped fresh herbs, such as chives (optional)

Method
Preheat the oven to 190°C/375°F/Gas 5. Bake pastry blind (page 230). Fill with the broccoli, tomatoes and half the cheese. Mix together the eggs and cream, season well, and add the herbs (if using). Pour into the pastry case. Sprinkle with the remaining cheese and bake in the oven for 35–45 minutes.

Mushroom Quiche
Serves 3–4
V

Ingredients
> 300g Nutty Pastry (page 230)
> small knob of butter
> 200g mushrooms, sliced
> 75g cheese, grated
> 2 eggs, beaten
> 125ml carton single cream
> salt and pepper
> few chopped fresh herbs, such as chives (optional)

Method
Preheat the oven to 190°C/375°F/Gas 5. Bake pastry blind (page 230). Melt the butter and fry the mushrooms gently for 1–2 minutes. Put in the pastry case with half the cheese and the herbs (if using). Beat together the eggs and cream, season and pour into the pastry case. Sprinkle with the remaining cheese and bake in the preheated oven for 35–45 minutes.

Pizza Dough
Enough to make 1 × 30cm pizza
V Ve

Ingredients
    200g strong white bread flour
    1 teaspoon salt
    1 teaspoon sugar
    1 teaspoon easy blend yeast
    1 teaspoon (5ml) oil

Method
Mix all the ingredients together, add 125ml hand-hot water, then knead for 5 minutes. Leave the dough to rise in a covered bowl for 45 minutes. Before using, knead once more until smooth.

Quick Pizza
Serves 4
V

Ingredients
    400g can chopped tomatoes
    1 tablespoon (15ml) tomato purée
    sprinkling of oregano
    2 large pizza bases
    6 mini cheeses from the pick 'n' mix section,
      or 100–150g cheese
    2 tablespoons sweetcorn
    2 tablespoons pineapple pieces
    black pepper

Method
Preheat the oven to 230°C/450°F/Gas 8. Simmer the tomatoes, tomato purée and oregano for 10–15 minutes until you have a thick sauce. Divide this between the pizza bases, coating them evenly. Slice the cheese over the tomato mixture, then top with the sweetcorn and pineapple. Bake in the preheated oven for 12–15 minutes.

Pizza Casa
Serves 2–4
V

We visited Italy this year. (The last time I had been there was on a Eurorail ticket – which I no longer qualify for.) We stayed in beautiful Ravello, where I was overcome by the quality of the fresh produce. This simple pizza was inspired by our stay there.

Ingredients
     1 quantity Pizza Dough (page 232)
     1 quantity Tomato Sauce (below)
     few basil leaves, shredded
     4 sun-dried tomatoes, sliced
     75g mozzarella, grated
     salt and pepper

Method
Preheat the oven to 200°C/400°F/Gas 6. Roll the dough out into a 30cm circle. Place on a large baking sheet and prick all over with a fork. Spread with the tomato sauce. Arrange the basil leaves and sun-dried tomatoes on top and sprinkle with the cheese. Season with salt and pepper. Bake in the pre-heated oven for 25–35 minutes.

Tomato Sauce *(for pizza)*
Makes enough to cover 1 × 30cm pizza
V Ve

Ingredients
     1 tablespoon (15ml) oil
     1 garlic clove, crushed
     400g can chopped tomatoes
     1 tablespoon (15ml) tomato purée

Method
Heat the oil and gently fry the garlic for 1 minute. Add the remaining ingredients and simmer gently until you have a thick sauce (approximately 20 minutes). It should be thick enough so that, when a spoon is pushed through it, you can see the bottom of the pan and the sauce remains separated.

Tomato and Aubergine Sauce *(for pasta)*
Serves 4
✳ **V Ve**

Ingredients
    1 onion, chopped
    2 cloves garlic, crushed
    3 tablespoons (45ml) oil
    1 aubergine, diced
    400g can chopped tomatoes
    1 tablespoon (15ml) tomato purée
    sprinkling of oregano
    salt and pepper

Method
Fry the onion and garlic in 1 tablespoon (15ml) of the oil for 5 minutes, add the aubergine and the remaining oil and continue to cook until soft (5–10 minutes). Add the rest of the ingredients and seasoning and simmer gently for 30 minutes. Serve with pasta.

Creamy Lentil Sauce *(for pasta)*
Serves 4
◔ **V**

Ingredients
    150g split red lentils
    1 teaspoon (5ml) Marmite
    2 onions, finely chopped
    2 cloves garlic, crushed
    200g mushrooms, chopped
    2 tablespoons (30ml) oil
    125g lite cream cheese, garlic and herb flavour
    2 tablespoons fresh parsley, chopped

Method
Put the lentils and Marmite in a small saucepan and cover with boiling water. Boil for 10 minutes, topping up with boiling water as necessary. Fry the onions, garlic and mushrooms in the oil until nicely golden. When the lentils have been reduced to a medium-thick purée, add the vegetables, cream cheese and parsley. Stir to heat through and serve with pasta.

Chick Peas with Banana and Mango
Serves 4
✳ ◔ **V**

This is a dish I'm surprised I haven't thought of before – it's just so incredibly quick and easy to make and utterly delicious.

Ingredients
>   2 x 430g cans chick peas, drained
>   4 bananas, thickly sliced
>   340g jar hot and spicy mango chutney
>   300g natural Greek-style yogurt

Method
Place all the ingredients in a saucepan and heat gently. Do not boil. When heated through thoroughly, serve with rice.

Aubergine, Mushroom and Coriander Balti
Serves 2
✳ ◔ **V Ve**

Balti paste has made it much easier to prepare home made curries in only a few minutes. This is currently one of our favourite recipes.

Ingredients
>   1 aubergine, diced
>   4 tablespoons (60ml) oil
>   100g mushrooms, sliced
>   1 onion, sliced
>   1 clove garlic, crushed
>   5 tablespoons (75g) balti paste
>   2 tablespoons chopped fresh coriander

Method
Fry the aubergine in the oil for 5–6 minutes, then add the mushrooms, onion and garlic, and continue cooking for a further 5 minutes. Stir in the balti paste and stir-fry for 5 minutes. Finally, mix in the coriander and serve.

Veggie Bolognese and Polenta
Serves 2
🕐 **V Ve**

Ingredients
    120g packet Beanfeast, bolognese style
    400g can chopped tomatoes
    225g instant polenta
    1 teaspoon salt

Method
Put the Beanfeast, tomatoes and 500ml water into a large saucepan. Bring to the boil and then simmer gently for 15 minutes. Bring 750ml water to the boil and add the polenta and salt. Stir with a wooden spoon while cooking for 5–10 minutes. Serve with the bolognese beans.

Ratatouille
Serves 4
✳ **V Ve**

Ingredients
    2 tablespoons (30ml) oil
    1 onion, chopped
    2 cloves garlic, chopped
    1 red pepper, chopped
    2 courgettes, chopped
    1 aubergine, chopped
    400g can chopped tomatoes with basil
    black pepper

Method
Heat the oil and fry the onion, garlic and pepper for 10 minutes. Add the courgettes and aubergine and cook for a further 10 minutes. Pour in the tomatoes and season with black pepper. Cover and simmer gently for 40 minutes. Can be served hot or cold.

Oven-baked Ratatouille
Serves 4
V Ve

I think ratatouille is best served just warm but it can also be served cold as a salad. I have found that this makes a great filling for lasagne as well (page 239).

Ingredients
> 200g courgette, sliced
> 200g aubergine, diced
> 1 orange pepper, diced
> 1 yellow pepper, diced
> 1 red onion, sliced
> 4 tomatoes, cut into wedges
> 4 tablespoons (60ml) oil
> salt and pepper

Method
Preheat the oven to 220°C/425°F/Gas 7. Mix everything together, making sure that the vegetables are well coated with oil. Spread over a roasting or baking tray and bake in the preheated oven for 40 minutes until the vegetables are starting to crisp at the edges. Serve warm or cold with rice or pasta.

Cheese and mushroom cannelloni
Serves 4
V

Ingredients
  2 tablespoons (30ml) oil
  2 onions, diced
  200g mushrooms, diced
  2 cloves garlic, crushed
  250g tub ricotta cheese
  100g cheese, grated
  12 cannelloni pasta tubes
  400ml Cheese Sauce (page 270)
  2 tablespoons (30ml) tomato purée
  sprinkling of oregano
  1 tablespoon (15ml) oil
  1 tablespoon (15ml) chilli sauce (optional)

Method
Preheat the oven to 200°C/400°F/Gas 6. Heat the oil and fry
the onions, mushrooms and garlic for 10 minutes. Stir in the
ricotta and half the grated cheese. Use this mixture to stuff
the cannelloni tubes. Pour half the cheese sauce into a
greased lasagne dish and arrange the tubes on top. Mix
together the tomato purée, oregano, 2 tablespoons (30ml)
water, the oil and chilli sauce (if using), and spread over the
rolls. Spoon the rest of the cheese sauce on top and sprinkle
with the remaining cheese. Bake in the preheated oven for
35 minutes until brown on top.

Ratatouille-filled Lasagne Rolls
Serves 4–6
V

Ingredients
    12 sheets fresh lasagne
    Oven-baked Ratatouille (page 237)
    500ml Cheese Sauce (page 270)
    75g cheese, grated

Method
Preheat the oven to 180°C/350°F/Gas 4. Soak the lasagne in boiling water for 5 minutes, then drain. Lay out the pasta and divide the ratatouille between the sheets, spreading it evenly over them. Roll the pasta up around the ratatouille and place the rolls in a lasagne dish. Cover with the cheese sauce and sprinkle with the cheese. Bake in the preheated oven for 30 minutes.

Undercover Beans (chilli version)
Serves 4
V

This is delicious! Tortilla chips make a great topping for casseroles and we are using them more and more. It doesn't matter what size packet you get, you can use the rest for nibbles before dinner.

Ingredients
> 3 tablespoons (45ml) oil
> 1 onion, chopped
> 2 cloves garlic, crushed
> 100g mushrooms, sliced
> 200g aubergine, diced
> 400g can chopped tomatoes
> 2 x 440g cans beans in chilli sauce
> packet tortilla chips
> 150ml carton sour cream
> 75g cheese, grated

Method
Preheat the oven to 180°C/350°F/Gas 4. Heat the oil and fry the onion, garlic and mushrooms for 2–3 minutes. Add the aubergine and continue to fry for 5 minutes. Transfer to a casserole dish and add the tomatoes and beans in chilli sauce. Cover and cook in the preheated oven for 45 minutes. Remove from the oven. Spread a layer of tortilla chips over the surface of the mixture, pour the cream on top and sprinkle with the cheese. Return the casserole dish to the oven and continue cooking, uncovered, for 15 minutes.

Cheese 'n' Lentil Bake
Serves 3–4
V

Ingredients
200g split red lentils
375ml vegetable stock *or* boiling water with 1
    teaspoon (5ml) Marmite
knob of butter
1 onion, diced
100g cheese, grated
salt and pepper

Method
Preheat the oven to 190°C/375°F/Gas 5. Cook the lentils in
the stock or boiling water until tender (15–20 minutes),
adding more water if needed. You want to end up with a
thick purée. Meanwhile, melt the butter and cook the onion
until it starts to colour. When the lentils are cooked, mash
with the grated cheese and onion. Season. Place in a
greased, lined 1kg loaf tin. Cook in the preheated oven for
50–60 minutes. Allow to cool in the tin for 5–10 minutes and
then serve.

Lentil and courgette bake
Add 1 large grated courgette to the lentil mixture before
baking.

Tomato and cheese topped bake
Instead of cooking the mixture in a loaf tin, put in a lasagne
or casserole dish and top with slices of tomato and more
grated cheese. Bake for 40–50 minutes.

Parsley and lentil bake
Add 1 tablespoon (15ml) crème fraîche, a squeeze of lemon
juice and 1 tablespoon chopped fresh parsley to the lentil
mixture before baking.

Vegetable and Bread Bake
Serves 4
V

You should be able to buy ready prepared bags of mixed vegetables for stews. If you cannot find these, then make your own mix from carrots, turnips, parsnips and swedes.

Ingredients
2 tablespoons (30ml) oil
1 onion, chopped
1kg mixed stew vegetables, chopped
1 teaspoon oregano
1 teaspoon thyme
295g can condensed cream of onion soup
400g can cannellini beans
black pepper
3–4 slices bread, well buttered
1 teaspoon (5ml) French mustard

Method
Preheat the oven to 200°C/400°F/Gas 6. Heat the oil and fry the onion and stew vegetables for 5 minutes. Remove from heat, add the oregano, thyme and 125ml boiling water, return to the boil and simmer for 10 minutes. Now mix in the soup and beans, and season with black pepper. Pour into a casserole dish and cover with the sliced bread, buttered side up. Dot with the mustard and bake in the preheated oven for 30 minutes.

Mexican Chilli Casserole
Serves 4
V

I found Vegemince in the freezer of a large supermarket; if you cannot find it use some diced vegetables or a dried variety of soya mince.

Ingredients
    2 tablespoons (30ml) oil
    1 onion, chopped
    1 red pepper, diced
    1 green pepper, diced
    450g Vegemince
    400g can chopped tomatoes
    400g can beans in chilli sauce
    150ml carton sour cream
    tortilla chips
    125g mozzarella cheese, grated

Method
Preheat the oven to 180°C/350°F/Gas 4. Heat the oil and fry the onion and peppers for 5 minutes. Add the Vegemince and stir to brown. Stir in the tomatoes and beans and pour into a large casserole dish. Cover and cook in the preheated oven for 1 hour. Remove from oven and top with the sour cream. Cover the surface with tortilla chips, then sprinkle with the cheese. Return to the oven and cook, uncovered, for 15 minutes.

Soya and Apple Casserole
Serves 3–4
✳ **V**

Always on the lookout for new products to try, I found these dried soya chunks in Sainsbury's. Although soya is in itself rather bland it does take on other flavours well. This is one of two recipes that I made with a pack.

Ingredients
   75g dried soya chunks
   2 tablespoons (30ml) oil
   1 onion, chopped
   1 green pepper, diced
   100g mushrooms, sliced
   400g cooking apples, cored, peeled and cut into thick
      slices
   2 tablespoons (30ml) tomato purée
   pinch of sage
   375ml dry cider *or* apple juice
   salt and pepper
   4 tablespoons (60ml) cream (optional)

Method
Rehydrate the soya in boiling water for 10 minutes. Meanwhile, heat the oil and fry the onion and pepper for 7 minutes. Add the mushrooms and apple and stir-fry for 3 minutes. Drain the soya and add to the mixture, with the tomato purée, sage and cider or apple juice. Season. Bring to the boil, cover and simmer for 20 minutes. Stir in the cream (if using) and serve.

Soya and Bean Goulash
Serves 3–4
✳ **V**

Ingredients
- 75g dried soya chunks
- 2 tablespoons (30ml) oil
- 2 onions, chopped
- 2 cloves garlic, crushed
- 1 red pepper, diced
- 1 green pepper, diced
- 400g can chopped tomatoes
- 400g can red kidney beans in chilli sauce
- extra chilli powder *or* sauce (optional)
- natural yogurt (to serve)

Method
Pour boiling water over the soya chunks and leave for 10 minutes. Heat the oil and fry the onions, garlic and peppers for 10 minutes. Drain the soya and add to the mixture, together with the tomatoes and kidney beans. Bring to the boil, cover and simmer for 20 minutes. Add extra chilli if required. Serve topped with yogurt.

Beer Fondue
Serves 2
✳ ⊕ **V**

My brother introduced me to this version and it is now just as popular as our original wine-based fondue. I like to use Ruddles beer, but I'm sure whichever your favourite beer is, will do! It's a strange thing that, considering how popular fondue sets used to be (almost *de rigueur* on wedding lists), I don't know many people who actually cook fondues. If you're lucky you may be able to borrow one from your parents' cupboard – after all if they never use it, why not let you have it?

Ingredients
> 250ml beer
> 250g cheese, grated
> 1 clove garlic, crushed
> 1 tablespoon cornflour, mixed with a little cold water
> 25g butter
> 1 teaspoon (5ml) French mustard
> French bread (for serving)

Method
Place the beer, cheese and garlic in a saucepan. Heat gently until the cheese melts. Add the cornflour mixture, butter and mustard. Keep stirring until the fondue thickens and bubbles. Serve in bowls with French bread to dip into the fondue.

11 The Blow-out Sunday Lunch

This is often the occasion that brings people to cook together for the first time. It needs some organisation. You must decide how many you are cooking for, what the menu is going to be, make out your shopping list, do the shopping, the cooking and, last but not least, the washing up! Once it is decided who will do what, this is much easier to organise than it sounds. Another option is that each person is totally responsible for one dish. But if you are doing it this way, you still need to make sure that everyone knows how much they have spent, so that you can add up the expenses and divide the total among you, to ensure that the person doing the main dish doesn't bear the brunt of the cost. I know some people prefer this second method but it can run into more problems ... If someone doesn't get up in time, for instance, you may find yourself without some of your lunch!

Still, it is one of the pleasures of life to be able to sit down with some friends and a bottle or two and really pig out. The afternoon should be kept free as the stupor produced by these meals usually entails a siesta!

I remember one afternoon when some of us had booked a court to play badminton . . . What a waste of money! When the time came, nobody wanted to go and we couldn't bring ourselves to run about the court. We all stood about moaning 'yours' as the shuttlecock passed us by. A big mistake!

Menu 1

Nut Roast
Tomato Sauce
Grilled Cheesy Mash
French Peas
Lemon and Banana Meringue Pie
Drink: red wine

Cooking hints

It is easiest to cook the pie first and serve it cold. If you want to serve it hot, don't forget to turn up the temperature of the oven when you take out the nut roast.

Nut Roast
Serves 6–8
V

This nut roast serves 6–8 so you will have enough for second helpings or to serve some cold the next day.

Ingredients
> 600g parsnips, chopped
> 2 tablespoons (30ml) oil
> 1 onion, chopped
> 2 celery sticks, chopped
> 1 clove garlic, crushed
> 100g mushrooms, chopped
> 25g butter
> 1 tablespoon fresh parsley
> pinch of dried thyme
> salt and pepper
> 150g peanuts, chopped
> 50g roasted hazelnuts
> 100g fresh breadcrumbs
> 1 egg, beaten

Method
Preheat the oven to 200°C/400°F/Gas 6. Cook the parsnips in boiling water until tender. While they are cooking, heat the oil and fry the onion, celery, garlic and mushrooms until soft. When the parsnips are cooked, drain and mash them with the butter. Mix all the ingredients together. Pour into a greased 1kg loaf tin. Cover with foil and cook in the preheated oven for 1–1¼ hours until the roast is firm to the touch. Leave to stand in the tin for 10 minutes before serving.

Tomato Sauce *(for nut roasts)*
Serves 3–4
✳ ⏱ **V Ve**

If you are serving nut roast just warm or cold then the best accompaniment is a tasty tomato sauce. This is our favourite – and can of course be used with other dishes as well. Passata can be found alongside tomato purée in supermarkets.

Ingredients
>2 tablespoons (30ml) oil
>1 onion, chopped
>400g can *or* packet of passata
>1 teaspoon sugar
>2 tablespoons (30ml) wine vinegar

Method
Heat 1 tablespoon (15ml) of the oil and fry the onion for 5 minutes until soft. Add the remaining ingredients and simmer for 5 minutes.

Grilled Cheesy Mash
Serves 3–4
V

Ingredients
>800g large potatoes, peeled and cut into large cubes
>knob of butter
>2 tablespoons (30ml) milk
>1 teaspoon mustard powder
>100g cheese, grated
>salt and pepper

Method
Cook the potatoes in boiling water until soft – about 20 minutes. Drain well. Preheat the grill. Mash the potatoes with the butter, milk, mustard powder and half the cheese. Season well. Put into a shallow, heatproof dish and sprinkle with the rest of the cheese. Grill until the cheese melts and starts to bubble and brown. Serve immediately.

French Peas
Serves 3–4
✳ ◔ **V**

Ingredients
> 400g frozen peas
> 1 dessertspoon sugar
> few leaves from a little gem lettuce, shredded
> 2–3 spring onions, finely chopped
> melted butter (to serve)

Method
Cook the peas, adding the sugar to the water. When cooked, add the lettuce and onions and leave for 1 minute. Drain and serve with butter.

Lemon and Banana Meringue Pie
Serves 4
V

This recipe came about because I had a banana which needed using up. I don't know why I hadn't thought of this combination before – it is utterly wonderful.

Ingredients
> 3 dessertspoons cornflour
> grated rind and juice of 2 lemons
> 175g caster sugar
> 2 eggs, separated
> 1 sweet pastry shell
> 1 banana, sliced

Method
Preheat the oven to 220°C/425°F/Gas 7. Blend the cornflour with 125ml water and put in a small saucepan with the grated rind and juice of the lemons. Bring to the boil, stirring. Reduce the heat and add 100g of the sugar, stirring until it has dissolved. Remove from the heat and cool slightly. Beat the egg yolks and add them to the lemon mixture. Arrange the banana in the bottom of the pastry shell and spoon the lemon mixture over before levelling the top. Whisk the egg whites with half the remaining sugar. When stiff, fold in the remaining sugar and pile on to the lemon mixture, completely covering the lemon base. Bake in the preheated oven for 10–15 minutes until the meringue is crisp and slightly browned.

> **Menu 2**
>
> Vegetable and Bean Gratin
> Baked Basmati Rice
> Leaf Salad
> Rhubarb Charlotte
> Drink: wine or cider

Cooking hints

Turn up the temperature of the oven when the main course is served and put in the pud 30 minutes before you wish to eat it.

Vegetable and Bean Gratin
Serves 4
V

Ingredients
2 aubergines, sliced
3 tablespoons (45ml) oil
1 onion, chopped
2 cloves garlic, chopped
400g can chopped tomatoes
1 tablespoon (15ml) tomato purée
100g chestnut mushrooms, thinly sliced
195g jar Pastasciutta with artichokes
400g can flageolet beans
75g fresh wholemeal breadcrumbs
50g Parmesan cheese

Method
Preheat the grill. Place the aubergine slices on foil under the preheated grill and brush with some of the oil. Cook until brown. Turn, brush with oil and grill the other side. Preheat the oven to 180°C/350°F/Gas 4. Heat the remaining oil and fry the onion and garlic for about 10 minutes, until soft and golden. Add the tomatoes and tomato purée and continue to cook until you have a thick sauce. Pour half the sauce into an ovenproof dish. Cover with half the aubergine slices. Add the mushrooms, artichokes and beans. Top with the rest of the tomato sauce and aubergine slices. Mix together the breadcrumbs and Parmesan and use to cover the vegetables. Bake in the preheated oven for 60 minutes.

Baked Basmati Rice
Serves 4–6
V Ve

Ingredients
400g basmati rice
600ml vegetable stock

Method
Preheat the oven to 180°C/350°F/Gas 4. Put the rice in a shallow casserole dish and pour in the stock. Cover the dish with foil and cook in the preheated oven for 35–45 minutes. (Cooking time will depend on the shape of your dish and how tightly it is covered.) Fluff the rice up with a fork before serving.

Leaf Salad
Serves 4–6
❋ ◔ **V Ve**

Ingredients
2 little gem lettuces, shredded
¼ iceberg lettuce, sliced
1 avocado, peeled, stoned and cubed
8 radishes, thinly sliced
½ cucumber, diced

For the dressing
6 tablespoons (90 ml) oil
2 tablespoons (30ml) orange juice
1 tablespoon (15ml) red wine vinegar
pinch of salt
1 teaspoon (5ml) whole-grain mustard

Method
Arrange the salad ingredients in a serving bowl. Put all the
dressing ingredients into a screw-top bottle or jar, shake
vigorously and pour over the salad just before serving.

Rhubarb Charlotte
Serves 4
V

Ingredients
>   75g butter
>   450g rhubarb, cleaned and cubed
>   150g fresh wholemeal breadcrumbs
>   1 teaspoon mixed spices
>   50g brown sugar
>   2 tablespoons (30ml) orange juice
>   2 tablespoons (30ml) runny honey
>   cream *or* custard (to serve)

Method
Preheat the oven to 200°C/400°F/Gas 6. Melt half the butter and fry the rhubarb until soft. Remove from the pan. Fry the breadcrumbs in the remaining butter until the butter is absorbed and the crumbs are browning. Layer the rhubarb and breadcrumbs in an ovenproof dish, finishing with a layer of crumbs. Mix the rest of the ingredients together and spoon over the dish. Bake in the preheated oven for 20 minutes and serve with cream or custard. Scrumptious!

```
┌─────────────────────────────────────────────┐
│ Menu 3                                        │
│ Summer Vegetable Bake                         │
│ Roasted New Potatoes with Rosemary            │
│ Carrots with Lemon and Ginger                 │
│ Brioche and Marmalade Pudding                 │
│ Drink: white wine                             │
└─────────────────────────────────────────────┘
```

Cooking hints

Put the pud in when you take the main course out of the oven.

Summer Vegetable Bake
Serves 4
V

Ingredients
> 25g butter
> 1 clove garlic, crushed
> 1 aubergine, sliced
> 1 tablespoon (15ml) oil
> 2 onions, finely chopped
> 1 yellow pepper, sliced
> 400g can chopped tomatoes
> 2 courgettes, halved and sliced
> 250g mushrooms, sliced
> 1 tablespoon Parmesan cheese

Method
Preheat the grill. Melt the butter, mix with the garlic and use to coat the aubergine slices. Grill for 4–5 minutes on each side until nicely brown. Preheat the oven to 180°C/350°F/ Gas 4. Heat the oil and fry the onions and pepper for 10 minutes until brown. Put half the tomatoes into an ovenproof dish. Add the courgettes, mushrooms and cooked onions and pepper. Cover with the aubergine slices, and then top with the remaining tomatoes and sprinkle with the Parmesan. Bake in the preheated oven for 45 minutes.

Roasted New Potatoes with Rosemary
Serves 4
V Ve

Ingredients
> 450g new potatoes, unpeeled
> 2 tablespoons (30ml) oil
> 1 tablespoon rosemary, chopped
> 1 clove garlic, crushed

Method
Preheat the oven to 180°C/350°F/Gas 4. Cook the potatoes for 5 minutes in boiling water, drain and put into a bowl. Pour in the oil, add the rosemary and garlic and stir to make sure the potatoes are well covered with the mixture. Place on a roasting tray and cook in the preheated oven for 30 minutes until browned.

Carrots with Lemon and Ginger
Serves 4
✳ ◷ **V**

Ingredients
> 400g carrots, in small chunks
> 2 teaspoons (10ml) ginger purée
> juice of 1 lemon
> 25g butter

Method
Cook the carrots in boiling water for 10–15 minutes until tender. Drain, add the remaining ingredients to the pan and cook until the butter is absorbed and the carrots are starting to brown.

Brioche and Marmalade Pudding
Serves 4–6
V

You can of course make this with bread instead of brioche – but since we tried it with brioche we have never gone back to using bread.

Ingredients
> 4 brioche rolls
> 75–100g butter, softened
> 3 tablespoons marmalade
> 400ml milk
> 3 eggs, beaten

Method
Preheat the oven to 180°C/350°F/Gas 4. Slice the brioche rolls and spread them with the butter. Place half the slices in an ovenproof dish and cover with the marmalade. Then top with the remaining brioche slices, buttered side up. Beat together the milk and eggs and pour over the brioche, pushing the slices down into the milk mixture. Bake in the preheated oven for about 30–40 minutes until well risen and brown.

```
┌─────────────────────────────────────────┐
│  Menu 4                                   │
│                                           │
│  Aubergine Dupiaza                        │
│  Bombay Potatoes                          │
│  Cauliflower in Nut Cream Sauce           │
│  Chillied Peas                            │
│  Cucumber Raita                           │
│  Indian bread                             │
│  Ice-cream or sorbet                      │
│  Drink: lager                             │
└─────────────────────────────────────────┘
```

Cooking hints

If you are cooking all this on your own I suggest you put your oven on to 150°C/300°F/Gas 2, so that you can keep some dishes warm while you are cooking others. Start by preparing the cucumber raita. Then go on to the cauliflower and potato dishes. Prepare the coconut, onion and cauliflower, then precook the potatoes. Now do the chillied peas and aubergine dupiaza (do not add the third onion and coriander to the aubergine yet). Put the chillied peas and aubergine dupiaza into the oven while cooking the Bombay potatoes and cauliflower in nut cream sauce. Finish off the aubergine. The Indian bread may need heating in the oven or grilling; check the pack/s. Choose a simple ice-cream or sorbet. You will want something refreshing, not rich, at the end of the meal. I suggest vanilla or coconut ice-cream, or lemon or passionfruit sorbet.

Aubergine Dupiaza
Serves 4
V

Ingredients

> 1 aubergine, sliced
> 4 tablespoons (60ml) oil
> 3 large onions
> 2 cloves garlic, crushed
> 1 teaspoon (5ml) ginger purée
> 2 tablespoons (30ml) balti paste
> 250g natural yogurt
> knob of butter
> 1 teaspoon brown sugar
> sprinkling of coriander

Method

Preheat the grill. Put the aubergine slices on foil under the preheated grill, brush with some of the oil and grill until brown. Turn and repeat. Chop 2 of the onions. Heat the remaining oil and cook the 2 onions, garlic and ginger for 10 minutes. Add the balti paste and stir-fry for 2 minutes. Add the aubergine and yogurt and stir to heat through. Slice the third onion. Melt the butter in a small frying pan, add the sugar and fry the onion until very brown. Pour the aubergine mixture into a bowl, pile the fried onion on top, sprinkle with coriander and serve.

Bombay Potatoes
Serves 4
⊕ **V   Ve**

Ingredients

> 200g new potatoes, halved
> 6 tablespoons (90ml) oil
> 1 tablespoon Bombay spices

Method

Boil the potatoes for 5 minutes, drain and pat dry. Heat the oil and fry the spices for 1 minute, and then add the potatoes. Stir-fry for a few minutes until brown.

Cauliflower in Nut Cream Sauce
Serves 4
V

Ingredients
> 4 tablespoons desiccated coconut
> 1 cauliflower, divided into florets
> 2 tablespoons (30ml) oil
> 1 onion, chopped
> 2 cloves garlic, crushed
> 2 tablespoons (30ml) balti paste
> 50g ground almonds
> 125ml carton double cream

Method
Put the coconut in a small bowl, just cover with boiling water and leave to stand for 30 minutes. Cook the cauliflower in boiling water for 5 minutes, then drain. Heat the oil and fry the onion and garlic for 5 minutes. Add the balti paste and stir-fry for 2 minutes. Add the cooked cauliflower and remaining ingredients and stir to heat through.

Chillied Peas
Serves 2–4
✳ ⊕ **V Ve**

Ingredients
>1 tablespoon (15ml) oil
>1 onion, chopped
>1 clove garlic, crushed
>2 teaspoons (10ml) balti paste
>chilli powder or sauce to taste
>100g frozen peas
>200g can chopped tomatoes

Method
Heat the oil and fry the onion and garlic for 5 minutes. Add the balti paste, chilli and peas and stir-fry for 2 minutes. Pour in the tomatoes. Bring to the boil, then cover and simmer for 10 minutes.

If serving this as the only vegetable, this quantity would really only stretch to two people.

Cucumber Raita
Serves 4
✳ ⊕ **V**

Ingredients
>¼ cucumber, finely diced
>2 spring onions, sliced
>2 tablespoons chopped fresh mint
>250g natural yogurt

Method
Mix all the ingredients together and serve.

12 Classic Vegetarian Student Dishes

These are favourite dishes with students everywhere. Looking at them I think that one of the reasons for their popularity is that they are easy to make in quantity, and therefore great for entertaining. The other thing that strikes me is that, like a lot of student food, they are strongly flavoured. With their continuing popularity, these are good dishes to master as they will greatly improve your reputation as a cook!

Although I refer to these as 'classic', the recipes themselves are my current versions of the dishes. My cooking continues to change as I search for the 'perfect' recipes!

All these recipes can be altered to cater for different numbers. Just remember that if you require double the quantity it is often best to make the recipe twice rather than try to fit it into one large dish. Large quantities can take a lot longer to cook.

You can stretch your main dish to serve more people by serving salads, baked potatoes and garlic bread with it.

Spag No-bol
Serves 2
⊙ **V Ve**

A perennial favourite when entertaining a friend: what can be nicer than a bowl of spaghetti and a glass of wine? We love garlic bread with this dish (although a salad would be a healthier alternative). Why not compromise and serve a salad *and* garlic bread!

Ingredients
    50g split red lentils
    2 tablespoons (30ml) oil
    1 onion, sliced
    1 clove garlic, crushed
    100g mushrooms, chopped
    200g can chopped tomatoes
    1 tablespoon (15ml) tomato purée
    sprinkling of oregano
    150g spaghetti

Method
Cook the lentils in boiling water for 10 minutes. Heat the oil and fry the onion, garlic and mushrooms for 10 minutes until soft. Add to the lentils with the tomatoes, tomato purée and oregano. Simmer gently for 5–10 minutes. Meanwhile, cook the spaghetti in boiling water and when ready, drain and serve with the lentil mixture.

Garlic Bread
Serves 4–6
V

Ingredients
    1 French loaf
    100g butter, softened
    mixed herbs
    2 cloves garlic, crushed
    poppy seeds (optional)

Method
Preheat the oven to 200°C/400°F/Gas 6. Slice the loaf at about 2.5cm intervals to within 1cm of the base. Mix together the butter, herbs and garlic and use to spread into the cuts. Smear a little butter over the top of the loaf and sprinkle with poppy seeds (if using). Wrap in foil and cook in the preheated oven for 20–30 minutes. Serve hot.

Creamy Vegetable and Nut Curry
Serves 4
V

This has to be one of the best curries that I have ever made. Please try it as it is easy to make and very, very good.

Ingredients
  4 tablespoons desiccated coconut
  1 aubergine (200g), diced
  1 potato (200g), cut into matchsticks
  200g carrot, diced
  100g frozen peas
  3 tablespoons (45ml) oil
  1 onion, sliced
  2 cloves garlic, crushed
  2 tablespoons (30ml) balti paste
  1 tablespoon (15ml) tomato purée
  4 tablespoons ground almonds
  125ml carton double cream

Method
Put the coconut into a bowl and just cover with boiling water. Leave to stand for 30 minutes. Place the aubergine, potato, carrot and peas in a saucepan with 250ml boiling water. Cover and cook for 10 minutes until the vegetables are tender. Meanwhile, heat the oil and fry the onion and garlic for 5 minutes before adding the balti paste and tomato purée. Stir-fry for 2 minutes. Add the cooked vegetables to the onion mixture and simmer for 5 minutes. Mix the almonds with the coconut and add the nut mixture with the cream to the vegetables. Stir and cook gently for a few minutes to heat through. Serve.

Lasagne
Serves 4–8
V

Ingredients
    1 aubergine, sliced
    4 tablespoons (60ml) oil
    100g split red lentils
    2 red onions, chopped
    2 cloves garlic, crushed
    1 red pepper, chopped
    200g mushrooms, sliced
    400g can chopped tomatoes
    1 tablespoon (15ml) tomato purée
    sprinkling of oregano
    salt and pepper
    9 sheets lasagne
    400ml Cheese Sauce (page 270)
    25g Parmesan cheese
    50g cheese, grated

Method
Preheat the grill. Brush the aubergine with some of the oil and grill until brown. Turn over and repeat. Preheat the oven to 180°C/350°F/Gas 4. Put the lentils in a pan with just enough water to cover, boil for 10 minutes, then simmer for a further 5, topping up with boiling water as necessary. Heat the remaining oil and fry the onions, garlic and pepper for 5 minutes. Add the mushrooms and cook for 5 minutes before adding the tomatoes and tomato purée. Sprinkle with oregano and simmer for 5 minutes. Mix the drained lentils and vegetables together. Season. Put a layer of the vegetable mixture in a lasagne dish. Cover with 3 sheets of lasagne and then put a third of the cheese sauce over these. Repeat the process twice to use up all the ingredients. Sprinkle with both cheeses and bake in the preheated oven for 35 minutes.

Cheese Sauce
Makes 500ml
✳ ◷ **V**

To make 400ml for baking with, use only 350 ml milk to make a much thicker sauce.

Ingredients
  50g butter or margarine
  50g flour, sifted
  450ml milk
  100g grated cheese
  mustard to taste

Method
Melt the butter or margarine in a small saucepan and then remove from the heat. Add the flour, stir well and return to a gentle heat, stirring continuously. Add a little milk at a time, and keep stirring to keep lumps at bay. The mixture will be very thick at first – keep thinning it gradually with the milk. When all the milk has been added, keep stirring and cooking for 2 minutes. Add the cheese and mustard, and continue cooking until the cheese has melted.

Cream sauce
Omit the cheese and mustard and add a 125ml carton double cream. Season well with plenty of black pepper.

Mushroom sauce
Omit the cheese and mustard. Add 200g sliced fried mushrooms and 2 tablespoons (30ml) double cream.

Moussaka
Serves 4
V

Ingredients
2 aubergines, sliced
6 tablespoons (90ml) oil
2 onions, chopped
2 cloves garlic, crushed
400g mushrooms, chopped
600g can chopped tomatoes
3 tablespoons (45ml) tomato purée
sprinkling of oregano or mixed herbs
salt and pepper
2 eggs, beaten
200g Greek yogurt
125g cheese, grated

Method
Preheat the grill. Brush the aubergine slices with some of the oil. Grill until brown (about 4–5 minutes), turn over and repeat. (You may need to do this in batches if you have a small grill.) Preheat the oven to 200°C/400°F/Gas 6. Heat 1 tablespoon (15ml) of the oil and fry the onions and garlic for 5–10 minutes until starting to brown. In another pan fry the mushrooms in 1 tablespoon (15ml) of the oil until soft. When the fried vegetables are ready, combine in one saucepan with the tomatoes, tomato purée and herbs and season with salt and pepper. Simmer for 10 minutes. Into a lasagne dish put half the vegetable mixture and cover with half of the aubergine slices. Top with the rest of the vegetable mixture and the remaining aubergine slices. Beat together the eggs, yogurt and cheese, and spoon over the aubergine slices. Cook in the preheated oven for about 30 minutes until brown on top.

Goulash (By-election Slops)
Serves 4–6
V Ve

This is one of those classic student dishes that is trotted out time and time again as it is easy to make and also cheap to serve to large numbers of people. The reason for the title is that I first experienced it when we were having a late-night meal while waiting for some important by-election results. Strangely, I don't remember anything about the by-election, just the meal. This goulash was followed by extremely, and I do mean extremely, runny brie!

Ingredients
1.25kg mixed vegetables, such as carrots, courgettes,
   potatoes, aubergines, mushrooms, corn
3 tablespoons (45ml) oil
2 onions, chopped
2 cloves garlic, crushed
400g can chopped tomatoes
1 red and 1 green pepper, chopped
4 tablespoons (60ml) tomato purée
2 tablespoons paprika
salt and pepper

Method
Preheat the oven to 190°C/375°/Gas 5. Cut the vegetables into bite-sized pieces. Heat the oil and fry the onions and garlic for 5 minutes. Mix in the remaining ingredients and seasonings and transfer to a casserole dish. Bake in the preheated oven for 40 minutes or until all the vegetables are cooked.

Cassoulet (Mean Beans)
Serves 4
V

This recipe from *Mean Beans* is still going down a treat with us and other garlic fiends. We usually accompany it with . . . garlic bread! This is not a dish to serve to: a) vampires, b) people who don't like garlic, or c) people about to go out for a night on the town.

Ingredients
>   3 tablespoons (45ml) oil
>   2 onions, chopped
>   4 cloves garlic, crushed
>   2 x 400g cans cannellini beans, drained
>   2 tablespoons soft brown sugar
>   2 tablespoons (30ml) wine vinegar
>   1 tablespoon (15ml) treacle
>   1 tablespoon (15ml) mustard
>   1 teaspoon chilli powder

For the mean butter
>   2 tablespoons butter, softened
>   2 tablespoons (30ml) French mustard
>   2 tablespoons fresh parsley, chopped
>   2 cloves garlic, crushed

Method
Preheat the oven to 180°C/350°F/Gas 4. Heat the oil and fry the onions and garlic for 10 minutes. Put with the remaining ingredients (except for those for mean butter) into a casserole dish and pour in 250ml boiling water. Do not cover. Cook in the preheated oven for 1 hour. Just before serving, mix the mean butter ingredients together and stir into the beans.

Sue's Chilli
Serves 5–6
V Ve

My memories of the origins of this dish are vague. I do know
it had something to do with watching a horse race – the
Grand National? – but all I really remember is we sat on the
floor with a large saucepan in the middle, helping ourselves
and smothering the chilli in sour cream and tortilla chips.

Ingredients
    oil for frying
    1 large onion, chopped
    2 cloves garlic, crushed
    1 aubergine, diced
    1 green pepper, diced
    2 carrots, sliced
    150g mushrooms, sliced
    2 x 400g cans tomatoes
    2 x 400g cans beans in chilli sauce
    3 tablespoons (45ml) tomato purée
    1–3 teaspoons chilli powder, to taste
    salt and pepper

Method
Heat a little oil and fry the vegetables until soft. Heat up the
beans in a large saucepan and add the vegetables and
tomato purée. Add the chilli, season and simmer gently for
30 minutes. Serve with pitta bread, sour cream and tortilla
chips.

Chilli Sin Carne
Serves 4
✳ ⊙ **V**

Ingredients
> 2 tablespoons (30ml) oil
> 1 onion, chopped
> 1 clove garlic, crushed
> 1 green pepper, chopped
> 250g minced Quorn
> 2 tablespoons (30ml) tomato purée
> 400g can chopped tomatoes
> 400g can red kidney beans, drained
> 1 packet Old El Paso chilli mix

Method
Heat the oil and fry the onion, garlic and pepper until soft. Add the Quorn and continue to cook until brown. Add the remaining ingredients and mix well. Cover tightly and simmer gently for 15 minutes.

Pizza
Serves 2–4
V

Ingredients
> 1 quantity Pizza Dough (page 232)
> 1 quantity Tomato Sauce (page 233)
> few thin slices green pepper
> few thin slices red pepper
> 50g mushrooms, chopped
> 2 spring onions, sliced
> 50g mozzarella cheese, grated
> salt and pepper
> sprinkling of chilli flakes

Method
Preheat the oven to 200°C/400°F/Gas 6. Roll the dough out into a 30cm circle. Place on a large baking sheet. Prick all over with a fork. Spread with the tomato sauce. Arrange the vegetables on top and sprinkle with the cheese. Season to taste with salt, pepper and chilli flakes. Cook in the preheated oven for 25–35 minutes.

13 Dinner Parties

Although this is not an aspect of cooking that people generally consider when they think of student cooking, it is something that some students find very enjoyable. You don't have to be a gourmet chef to be able to cook for these dinner parties. These are tried and tested recipes which even those who have little experience can undertake. The menus I have chosen are varied and mirror meals that one would generally enjoy in restaurants – but at a fraction of the cost.

Organisation is the key to happy entertaining; check and double-check! Be particularly wary of assuming that you have an ingredient in your store cupboard only to discover at the last minute that what you actually have is an empty container.

I have arranged this chapter to make it as easy as possible for you. For each menu I have worked out a shopping list and a time plan. Just remember: a) if you are providing the drinks you need to add these to your shopping list (ditto coffee/milk if you are having them); b) the time plan is the preparation time *after* you have got everything ready, that is, chopped the vegetables, precooked items, etc. Only you can estimate how long that will take you.

Menu 1

Garlic Mushrooms
Stuffed Aubergines
Brown Rice
Salad
Squidgy Tart
Preparation time: 1 hour

Shopping list

375g mushrooms
5 cloves garlic
3 aubergines
2 red onions
80–100g pack of salad leaves
75g green lentils
300g easy cook brown rice
wine *or* sherry vinegar
olive oil
tomato purée
dried herbs

French mustard
100g good cooking
    chocolate
200g tiny marshmallows
1 sweet pastry shell
French bread
wine (optional)
250ml carton double cream
75g butter
salt and pepper

Time plan: to eat at 8:30

7.30   Make squidgy tart
7.40   Mix vinaigrette ingredients together
7.45   Prepare stuffed aubergines
8.20   Start garlic mushrooms
8.30   Put rice on to cook
       Put aubergines in oven
       Serve garlic mushrooms
Later: Dress salad just before serving

Garlic Mushrooms
Serves 6
🕐 **V**

This is my latest version of garlic mushrooms. I have started adding cream to this dish and I do think that this makes it even nicer. (Yes – and even more fattening. But as long as you don't eat it every day it won't hurt.)

Ingredients
300g mushrooms, quartered
3 cloves garlic, crushed
75g butter
6 slices French bread
1½ teaspoons (7.5ml) French mustard
3 tablespoons (45ml) double cream

Method
Preheat the grill. Melt the butter and cook the mushrooms and garlic for 3 minutes. Toast the bread. Add the mustard and cream to the mushroom mixture, heat through and serve on the toasted bread.

Stuffed Aubergines
Serves 6
V Ve

Ingredients
   75g green lentils
   2 red onions, chopped
   2 cloves garlic, crushed
   75g mushrooms, sliced
   5 tablespoons (75ml) olive oil
   3 tablespoons (45ml) tomato purée
   3 aubergines, halved and flesh scooped out and diced
   5 tablespoons (75ml) red wine *or* water
   salt and pepper

Method
Preheat the oven to 200°C/400°F/Gas 6. Boil the lentils in plenty of water for 10 minutes and then simmer for a further 20. Meanwhile, heat one-third of the oil and fry the onions, garlic and mushrooms until starting to brown. Remove from the pan. Reserve 1 tablespoon of the oil and 1 tablespoon of the tomato purée, heat the rest of the oil and then cook the aubergines for 5 minutes. Return the other vegetables to the pan and add the remaining 2 tablespoons (30ml) tomato purée and wine (or water). Stir and then remove from heat. Season well. When the lentils are cooked add them to the other ingredients. Use to stuff the aubergine shells. Mix the reserved oil and tomato purée and brush over shell edges. Place on a baking tray and bake in the preheated oven for 25 minutes.

Brown Rice
Serves 6
✳ ◴ **V Ve**

Ingredients
   300g easy cook brown rice

Method
Put the rice in a large saucepan with 750ml cold water. Cover and bring to the boil. Stir and replace lid. Simmer for 20–25 minutes, until all the water is absorbed.

Salad
Serves 6
✳ ☉ **V Ve**

Ingredients
    80–100g pack of salad leaves

    Vinaigrette
    3 tablespoons (45ml) olive oil
    1 tablespoon (15ml) wine *or* sherry vinegar
    pinch of dried herbs
    salt and pepper

Method
Mix all vinaigrette ingredients together and use to dress the salad. Serve immediately.

Squidgy Tart
Serves 6
✳

This is not a recipe for a strict vegetarian because if you look carefully at the ingredients on the marshmallow pack you will find gelatin. This came as a complete surprise to me, as I'd never suspected marshmallows of not being suitable for vegetarians. It just shows how careful you have to be if you are determined to exclude animal products completely from your diet.

Ingredients
    125ml carton double cream
    100g good cooking chocolate
    200g tiny marshmallows
    1 sweet pastry shell

Method
Put the double cream, chocolate and half the marshmallows into a saucepan and heat gently, stirring until melted. Pour into the pastry shell and top with the remaining marshmallows. Chill.

```
┌─────────────────────────────────────────────┐
│                                             │
│  Menu 2                                     │
│  Potato Skins and Sour Cream Dip            │
│  Vegeburgers                                │
│  Oven Chips                                 │
│  Salad with Banana Dressing                 │
│  Ice-cream with Chocolate Fudge Sauce       │
│  Preparation time: 1 hour                   │
│                                             │
└─────────────────────────────────────────────┘
```

Shopping list

4 x 250g potatoes
chives
punnet of mustard and cress
1 clove garlic (optional)
packet mixed lettuce leaves
1 white or red cabbage
1 yellow pepper
1 banana
oil
soy sauce
chilli powder

salt and pepper
jar chilli relish
white wine vinegar
honey
soft brown sugar
125ml carton sour cream
butter
4 chargrilled vegeburgers
500ml vanilla ice-cream
4 sesame seed burger buns
1 x 65g Mars bar

Time plan: to eat at 8:30

7.30   Measure out ingredients for fudge sauce
       Prepare salad and dressing (but don't add banana until
       you are ready to serve)
7.40   Prepare potato skins
       Preheat oven
7.50   Prepare oven chips
8.10   Put potato skins in oven
       Prepare dip
8.20   Put oven chips in oven
8.30   Turn down oven temperature
       Put in vegeburgers
       Serve potato skins and dip
8.50   Serve main course

Potato Skins
Serves 4
🕐 **V Ve**

Ingredients
>4 x 250g potatoes
>2 tablespoons (30ml) oil
>2 tablespoons (30ml) soy sauce
>pinch of chilli powder

Method
Preheat the oven to 220°C/425°F/Gas 7. Cut the skins from the potatoes thickly (the flesh will be used for the oven chips). Mix with the other ingredients. Put on a baking tray and cook in the preheated oven for about 20 minutes until crisp and brown. Serve with the dip (below).

Sour Cream Dip
Serves 4
✳ 🕐 **V**

Ingredients
>125ml carton sour cream
>2 tablespoons chopped chives
>salt and pepper
>1 clove garlic, crushed (optional)

Method
Combine all the ingredients, and pour into a small serving bowl.

Vegeburgers
Serves 4
🕐 **V**

I have never been that impressed with bought vegeburgers –
many are fairly tasteless and, even worse, tend to fall apart
when cooked. However, the chargrilled vegeburgers from Safe-
ways are the exception. We have been really impressed with
both their flavour and their texture. Well worth hunting out.

Ingredients
    4 chargrilled vegeburgers
    4 sesame seed burger buns
    3 tablespoons (45ml) chilli relish

Method
Preheat the oven to 180°C/350°F/Gas 4. Place the burgers on
a baking tray and cook in the preheated oven for 20 minutes,
turning once. Split the buns in half. When the burgers are
cooked, put one on each bun, top with the chilli relish and
cover with the remaining bun halves. Serve immediately.

Oven Chips
Serves 4
V Ve

Ingredients
    4 x 250g potatoes, skins removed
    2 tablespoons (30ml) oil
    salt

Method
Preheat the oven to 220°C/425°F/Gas 7. Cut the potatoes
into slices and then cut the slices into strips. Put into a
saucepan with cold water and bring to the boil. Cook for 3
minutes then plunge the potatoes into cold water. Drain and
pat dry. Mix with the oil and season with salt. Place on a
baking tray and cook in the preheated oven for 10 minutes.
Then turn down heat to 180°C/350°F/Gas 5 and bake for a
further 20–25 minutes until the chips have browned.

Salad with Banana Dressing
Serves 4
✳ ⊕ **V Ve**

Ingredients
> packet mixed lettuce leaves
> 100g white or red cabbage, thinly sliced
> 1 yellow pepper, chopped
> punnet of mustard and cress

For the banana dressing
> 4 tablespoons (60ml) oil
> 1 tablespoon (15ml) white wine vinegar
> 1 teaspoon (5ml) honey
> 1 banana, chopped finely
> salt and pepper

Method
Place the salad ingredients in a serving bowl. Combine all the dressing ingredients thoroughly and pour over the salad. Toss and serve immediately.

Ice-cream with Chocolate Fudge Sauce
Serves 4
✳ ⊕ **V**

This is utterly delicious and very popular in our household.

Ingredients
> 1 x 65g Mars bar, chopped
> 1 tablespoon butter
> 1 tablespoon soft brown sugar
> 500ml vanilla ice-cream

Method
Place a heatproof bowl over a small saucepan of boiling water. (Don't let it touch the water.) Put the Mars bar, butter and sugar in the bowl to melt. Then beat in 1 tablespoon (15ml) boiling water. When the sauce is smooth, pour over the ice-cream and serve.

Menu 3

Crudités with Garlic Dip
Fajitas
Salad, sour cream, grated cheese
Salsa
Guacamole
Chocolate Tiramisu
Preparation time: 1 hour

Shopping list

2 carrots
2 green peppers
2 red peppers
½ cucumber
½ cauliflower
6 cloves garlic
1 red onion
3 tomatoes
1 aubergine
1 small onion
1 lemon
1 large ripe avocado
salad leaves
soft cream cheese
125ml carton single cream
125ml carton sour cream

100g cheese
250g mascarpone cheese
eggs
mayonnaise
oil
chilli powder
ground coriander
8 tortillas
caster sugar
vanilla essence
coffee
230g can chopped tomatoes
tomato purée
miniature brandy
2 chocolate flakes
box sponge fingers

Time plan: to eat at 8:30

7.30   Prepare tiramisu
7.40   Prepare salsa
7.50   Prepare crudités
7.55   Prepare dip
8.00   Prepare guacamole
8.05   Prepare stuffing for tortillas (keep warm)
8.30   Serve crudités and dip
8.50   Serve main course

Crudités
Serves 4
✳ ◷ **V Ve**

Ingredients
>   2 carrots, cut into matchsticks
>   1 red pepper, cut into lengths
>   ½ cucumber, cut in half and then into lengths
>   ½ small cauliflower, divided into florets

Method
After you have prepared the vegetables, store them in a plastic bag in the salad drawer of the fridge to keep fresh. When ready to eat, serve with garlic dip.

Garlic Dip
Serves 4
✳ ◷ **V**

Ingredients
>   2 tablespoons soft cream cheese
>   2 tablespoons (30ml) single cream
>   2 tablespoons (30ml) mayonnaise
>   2 cloves garlic, crushed

Method
Mix all ingredients together thoroughly.

Cheese Dip
Serves 4
✳ ◷ **V**

If you want to serve different dips, remember to adjust your shopping list accordingly.

Ingredients
> 125g soft cream cheese
> 1 tablespoon soft margarine or butter
> 1 tablespoon (15ml) mayonnaise

Method
Blend together the cheese and margarine, and then stir in the mayonnaise.

Blue cheese dip
To the above, add some crushed blue cheese, such as Danish blue.

Cheese and tomato dip
To the main recipe, add 1 tablespoon (15ml) tomato ketchup or purée.

Tomato and Garlic Dip
Serves 4
✳ ◷ **V Ve**

Ingredients
> 2 tablespoons (30ml) tomato purée
> 1 tablespoon (15ml) oil
> 2 cloves garlic, crushed
> salt and pepper

Method
Mix all the ingredients together thoroughly with 2 table-spoons (30ml) hot water.

Fajitas
Serves 4
V Ve

Ingredients
>   8 tablespoons (120ml) oil
>   2 cloves garlic, crushed
>   1 aubergine, thinly sliced
>   1 red onion, sliced
>   1 red pepper, diced
>   1 green pepper, diced
>   2 tomatoes, skinned (page 231) and chopped
>   sprinkling of chilli powder
>   pinch of ground coriander
>   8 tortillas

Method
Mix together 6 tablespoons (90ml) of the oil and the garlic. Use to coat the aubergine and grill until brown. (Takes about 4–5 minutes each side.) Heat the remaining oil and fry the onion and peppers for 5 minutes. Then add the tomatoes, chilli and coriander and fry for a further 5 minutes. Mix all the vegetables together and use as a stuffing for the tortillas.

Fajitas are usually served with salad, grated cheese, sour cream and salsa.

Salsa
Serves 4–6
✳ ⏱ **V Ve**

Although you can now buy many varieties of salsa in the shops and some of them are very good, I still like to make my own. You can alter the heat of your salsa by varying the amount of chilli you use. You can also use chilli sauce rather than chilli powder if you prefer.

Ingredients
>2 tablespoons (30ml) oil
>½ green pepper, finely chopped
>1 small onion, finely chopped
>2 cloves garlic, crushed
>sprinkling of chilli powder
>230g can chopped tomatoes
>1 tablespoon (15ml) tomato purée

Method
Heat 1 tablespoon (15ml) of the oil and fry the pepper and onion for 5 minutes. Add the garlic, chilli and tomatoes and simmer gently for 5 minutes. Finally, add the rest of the oil and the tomato purée, stir and leave to cool.

Guacamole
Serves 4–6
✳ ⏱ **V Ve**

In our house this is a very popular dish. I often serve it with salsa and a sour cream dip and crudités and tortilla chips. My recipe often changes; this is the one we are using at the moment.

Ingredients
>1 large ripe avocado, peeled and stoned
>½ teaspoon (2.5ml) tomato purée *or* 1 chopped
>   tomato
>sprinkling of chilli or cayenne pepper
>squeeze fresh lemon juice

Method
Mash the avocado flesh to a smooth purée and then mix with the remaining ingredients. Serve with crudités or tortilla chips.

Chocolate Tiramisu
Serves 4–6
✳ ◔ **V**

Ingredients
    250g mascarpone cheese
    2 egg yolks, beaten
    2 tablespoons caster sugar
    1 teaspoon (5ml) vanilla essence
    200ml double-strength black coffee
    miniature brandy
    box sponge fingers
    2 chocolate flakes, crumbled

Method
Beat together the mascarpone cheese, egg yolks, caster sugar and vanilla essence. Mix together the coffee and brandy. Dip half the sponge fingers into the coffee mixture and arrange in a serving dish. Cover with half the mascarpone mixture and half the chocolate flake. Dip the remaining fingers in the coffee and arrange in another layer on top. Cover with the rest of the mascarpone mixture and sprinkle the rest of the chocolate over it. Chill before serving.

Menu 4

Pakoras
Mint, Coconut and Coriander Raita
Bean Dhansak
Mushroom and Coriander Bhajee
Bhindi Bhajee (okra curry)
Lemon Rice
Mango Cream
Preparation time: 1½ hours

Shopping list

1 cauliflower
1 pepper
15g packet mint leaves
2 x 15g packets coriander
   leaves
2 lemons
spring onions
7 cloves garlic
400g okra
400g mushrooms
1 aubergine
1 potato
200g carrots
4 onions
150ml carton natural yogurt
250ml carton double cream
desiccated coconut

150g basmati rice
plain flour
salt
garam masala
ginger purée
curry paste
balti paste
turmeric
oil
tomato purée
600g can chopped tomatoes
200g can chopped tomatoes
400g can red kidney beans
split red lentils
vegetable stock cube
400g can mango slices

Time plan: to eat at 8:30

7.00	Soak coconut for raita
7.05	Make mango cream
7.15	Make raita
7.25	Start bhindi bhajee
	Preheat oven to 150°C/300°F/Gas 2 to keep dishes warm as you cook them
7.35	Start bean dhansak
7.50	Start mushroom and coriander bhajee
8.05	Start cooking rice
8.10	Start making pakoras
8.30	Serve pakoras with raita
8.45	Serve main course

Pakoras
Serves 4
✳ ☾ **V Ve**

Ingredients
    100g plain flour
    pinch of salt
    1 teaspoon garam masala
    oil for frying
    6–8 cauliflower florets, halved
    1 pepper, sliced into rings

Method
Blend the flour, salt and garam masala with just enough water (about 125ml) to make a smooth batter. Pour enough oil into a pan to give a depth of 2.5cm and heat until very hot. Dip the vegetables into the batter and then fry a few pieces at a time for 5–6 minutes until golden brown.

Mint, Coconut and Coriander Raita
Serves 4
✳ ☾ **V**

Ingredients
    2 tablespoons desiccated coconut
    15g packet mint leaves, chopped
    15g packet coriander leaves, chopped (but reserve
        1 tablespoon for the bhindi bhajee)
    2–3 spring onions, chopped
    1 clove garlic, crushed
    1 teaspoon (5ml) ginger purée
    2 teaspoons (10ml) curry paste
    4 tablespoons (60ml) yogurt

Method
Mix the coconut with 3 tablespoons (45ml) boiling water and leave to soak for 15 minutes. Add the other ingredients, stir thoroughly and chill before serving.

Bean Dhansak
Serves 4
V Ve

Ingredients
- 1 aubergine (200g), diced
- 1 potato (200g), cut into matchsticks
- 200g carrots, diced
- 3 tablespoons (45ml) oil
- 1 onion, sliced
- 2 cloves garlic, crushed
- 200g mushrooms, sliced
- 1 teaspoon (5ml) ginger purée
- 2 tablespoons (30ml) balti paste
- 2 tablespoons (30ml) tomato purée
- 100g split red lentils
- 600g can chopped tomatoes
- 400g can red kidney beans, drained

Method
Cook the aubergine, potato and carrots in boiling water for 10 minutes, then drain. Heat 2 tablespoons (30ml) of the oil and fry the onion and garlic for 5 minutes until soft. Add the remaining oil and the mushrooms and continue to cook for 5 minutes. Add the ginger, balti paste and tomato purée. Fry for 3 minutes. Meanwhile, cook the lentils for 10 minutes in just enough boiling water to cover, topping up with water as necessary. Transfer all the ingredients except the beans to a large saucepan. Bring to the boil, cover and simmer for 15 minutes. Then add the beans and simmer for a further 5 minutes. Serve.

Mushroom and Coriander Bhajee
Serves 4
✳ ⏲ **V Ve**

Ingredients
  3 tablespoons (45ml) oil
  1 onion, chopped
  2 teaspoons garam masala
  2 cloves garlic, crushed
  1 tablespoon (15ml) tomato purée
  200g mushrooms, sliced
  15g packet coriander, chopped

Method
Heat the oil and fry the onion for 5 minutes, add the garam masala and garlic and cook for a further 2 minutes. Add the tomato purée and mushrooms and stir-fry for 4–5 minutes until the mushrooms are cooked. Add the coriander and stir before serving.

Bhindi Bhajee (Okra Curry)
Serves 4
✳ ⏲ **V Ve**

Ingredients
  6 tablespoons (90ml) oil
  450g okra, topped and tailed
  2 onions, chopped
  2 cloves garlic, crushed
  1 teaspoon (5ml) ginger purée
  2 tablespoons (30ml) balti paste
  200g can chopped tomatoes
  1 tablespoon (15ml) tomato purée
  1 tablespoon fresh coriander, chopped

Method
Heat the oil and fry the okra, onions and garlic for 5 minutes. Add the ginger and curry paste and cook for 3 minutes. Add the tomatoes and tomato purée. Cover and cook for 15 minutes. Stir in the coriander and serve.

Lemon Rice

Serves 4

✳ ◷ **V Ve**

Ingredients

    1 tablespoon (15ml) oil
    1 teaspoon turmeric
    rind of 2 lemons
    150g basmati rice
    375ml vegetable stock

Method

Heat the oil and fry the turmeric for 1 minute, add the lemon rind and the rice and stir. Pour in the vegetable stock, bring to the boil, cover and simmer for 10–12 minutes until the rice is cooked.

Mango Cream

Serves 4

✳ ◷ **V**

Ingredients

    400g can mango slices, drained
    250ml carton double cream

Method

Mash the mango slices to a smooth purée. Lightly whip the cream until it starts to hold its shape. Mix the mango purée and cream together, and pour into 4 small serving dishes. Chill.

Menu 5

Sweet 'n' Sour Vegetables
Tomato and Chilli Chow Mein
Stir-fried Broccoli and Cashews
Egg Fried Rice
Lychees and Mangoes
Preparation time: 30 minutes

Shopping list

1 green pepper
1 red pepper
1 carrot
2 celery sticks
100g mushrooms
200g broccoli
1 clove garlic
frozen peas
300g rice
oil
soy sauce
chilli sauce
tomato sauce

Chinese nest noodles
225g can bamboo shoots
160g jar sweet 'n' sour sauce
410g can mangoes
425g can lychees
50g unsalted cashews
ginger purée
sherry *or* white wine
cornflour
honey
1 egg
salt and pepper

Time plan: to eat at 8:30

8.00   Preheat oven to 150°C/300°F/Gas 2 to keep dishes warm as you cook them
Prepare lychees and mangoes
Put rice on to cook
8.10   Prepare sweet 'n' sour vegetables
8.15   Prepare stir-fried broccoli and cashews
Prepare noodles for chow mein
8.20   Prepare egg fried rice
8.25   Prepare tomato and chilli chow mein
8.30   Serve

Sweet 'n' Sour Vegetables
Serves 4
✳ ☉ **V Ve**

Ingredients
>   2 tablespoons (30ml) oil
>   1 green pepper, sliced
>   1 red pepper, sliced
>   1 carrot, cut into matchsticks
>   2 celery sticks, sliced
>   225g can bamboo shoots, drained
>   160g jar sweet 'n' sour sauce

Method
Heat the oil and stir-fry the peppers, carrot and celery for 2–3 minutes. Add the bamboo shoots and sweet 'n' sour sauce. Cook for 2 minutes and serve.

Tomato and Chilli Chow Mein
Serves 4
☉ **V Ve**

Ingredients
>   100g Chinese nest noodles
>   2 tablespoons (30ml) oil
>   100g mushrooms
>   50g frozen peas

For the sauce
>   2 tablespoons (30ml) soy sauce
>   1 tablespoon (15ml) chilli sauce
>   2 tablespoons (30ml) tomato sauce

Method
Cook the noodles until soft. Drain. Toss in 1 tablespoon of the oil. Stir-fry the mushrooms and peas in the remaining oil for 2 minutes. Pour in the sauce ingredients and cook for 1 minute. Add the noodles and stir through before serving.

Stir-fried Broccoli and Cashews
Serves 4
✳ ⊙ **V Ve**

Ingredients
>1 tablespoon (15ml) oil
>200g broccoli florets, sliced
>1 clove garlic, crushed
>1 teaspoon (5ml) ginger purée
>50g unsalted cashews

For the sauce
>1 teaspoon cornflour
>2 tablespoons (30ml) soy sauce
>2 tablespoons (30ml) sherry or white wine
>1 teaspoon (5ml) honey

Method
Heat the oil and stir-fry the broccoli, garlic and ginger for 2 minutes. Add the cashews and stir through. Dissolve the cornflour in 4 tablespoons (60ml) of water. Mix with the other sauce ingredients and add to the pan. Cook for 2 minutes. Serve.

Egg Fried Rice
Serves 4
✳ ⊙ **V**

Ingredients
>2 tablespoons (30ml) oil
>300g cooked rice
>1 egg, lightly beaten
>salt and pepper

Method
Heat the oil and stir-fry the rice, add the egg and continue to stir until the egg starts to set. Season well and serve.

Lychees and Mangoes
Serves 4
✳ ◔ **V Ve**

Ingredients
> 425g can lychees
> 410g can mangoes

Method
Drain both cans, reserving 4 tablespoons (60ml) syrup from the can of mangoes. Divide the fruit between 4 serving bowls and spoon some of the reserved juice over each. Serve.

14 Feeding the Loved One

These are recipes for those romantic *dîners à deux* to celebrate birthdays, Valentine's Day and other special occasions. You can also prepare them when you are trying to attract that special person into your life. Whether you go to town on the presentation – flowers, candles, etc. – depends on your own style and on how obvious you want your intentions to be!

If using wine in cooking you could get a measure from the student bar or a can from a supermarket or off-licence. The cans hold two measures (one for the dish, one for the cook!) This saves you having to open a bottle – which you would probably rather drink, or which could be difficult if it is your guest who is bringing the wine.

Menu 1

Pasta with Walnuts
Side Salad
Ricotta with Honey and Pine Nuts
Preparation time: 20 minutes

Shopping list

100g mushrooms
1 little gem lettuce
1 iceberg lettuce
bunch of spring onions
bunch of radishes
½ cucumber
1 clove garlic
pine nuts
50g chopped walnuts
150g pasta bows *or*
    tagliatelle

butter
80g Boursin
250g tub ricotta cheese
milk
salt and pepper
oil
wine vinegar
dried mustard powder
runny honey

Order of cooking

1. Prepare ricotta (do not sprinkle with nuts)
2. Prepare salad and dressing
3. Prepare and cook pasta
4. Dress salad and serve with pasta
5. Sprinkle ricotta with pine nuts and serve

Pasta with Walnuts
Serves 2
🕐 **V**

Ingredients
>150g pasta bows *or* tagliatelle
>25g butter
>100g mushrooms, sliced
>80g Boursin, garlic and herb flavoured
>4 tablespoons (60ml) milk
>50g chopped walnuts
>salt and pepper

Method
Cook the pasta as directed on the packet. Meanwhile, melt the butter and fry the mushrooms for 2–3 minutes. Add the Boursin and milk to the pan and gently melt down to make a sauce. Add the walnuts and heat through. Season well and serve with the pasta.

Side Salad
Serves 2
✳ ⏲ **V Ve**

Ingredients
>1 little gem lettuce, shredded
>few slices iceberg lettuce
>2–3 spring onions, sliced
>3–4 radishes, sliced
>7cm length of cucumber, sliced

For the dressing
>2 tablespoons (30ml) oil
>2 teaspoons (10ml) wine vinegar
>1 clove garlic, crushed
>pinch of salt
>pinch of dried mustard powder

Method
Place the salad ingredients in a bowl. Mix the dressing ingredients together and pour over the salad just before serving.

Ricotta with Honey and Pine Nuts
Serves 2
✳ ⏲ **V**

Ingredients
>3 teaspoons (15ml) runny honey
>250g tub ricotta cheese
>1 tablespoon pine nuts

Method
Mix 2 teaspoons (10ml) of the honey with the cheese and then divide between two bowls. Drizzle the remaining honey over the ricotta and sprinkle with the nuts.

Menu 2

Sweet Aubergine Stew
Buttered Rice
Raspberry Creams
Preparation time: 1 hour

Shopping list

1 red onion
1 clove garlic
200g mushrooms
1 red pepper
1 aubergine
100g raspberries
oil
125ml carton whipping
    cream

butter
100g basmati rice
lemon or ginger crisp biscuits
400g can chopped tomatoes
soft light brown sugar
red wine
salt and pepper

Order of cooking

1. Prepare and cook aubergine stew
2. Prepare raspberry creams
3. Soak basmati rice
4. 20 minutes before you wish to eat, cook rice

Sweet Aubergine Stew
Serves 2
V Ve

Ingredients
 2 tablespoons (30ml) oil
 1 red onion, chopped
 1 clove garlic, crushed
 200g mushrooms, quartered
 1 red pepper, diced
 200g aubergine, diced
 400g can chopped tomatoes
 1 dessertspoon soft light brown sugar
 125ml red wine
 salt and pepper

Method
Preheat the oven to 180°C/350°F/Gas 4. Heat the oil and fry the onion, garlic, mushrooms and pepper for 2–3 minutes. Add the aubergine and continue to fry for 5 minutes. Transfer to a casserole dish and add the tomatoes, sugar and red wine. Season. Cover and cook in the preheated oven for 50 minutes.

Buttered Rice
Serves 2
 ✳ ◷ **V**

Ingredients
 100g basmati rice
 25g butter

Method
Place the rice and half the butter in a pan with 250ml cold water. Bring to the boil, stir and cover. Simmer for 10–12 minutes until the water is absorbed. Fork the remaining butter into the rice before serving.

Raspberry Creams

Serves 2

✳ 🕐 **V**

Ingredients
> 100g raspberries
> 125ml carton whipping cream
> lemon *or* ginger crisp biscuits (to serve)

Method
Mash or purée the fruit – or sieve if preferred. I like the
texture you get when the fruit is just mashed. Whip the
cream until it holds its shape. Gently stir in the fruit and
divide between 2 bowls. Serve with some crisp lemon or
ginger biscuits.

Menu 3

Crunchy Stuffed Courgettes
Creamy Potatoes
Steamed Broccoli
Strawberries and Cream
Preparation time: 35 minutes

Shopping list

2 large courgettes
1 onion
100g mushrooms
200g new potatoes
200g punnet of strawberries
200g broccoli
oil
tomato purée

white wine *or* sherry
dried tarragon
roasted chopped hazelnuts
salt and pepper
butter
80g Boursin
milk
150ml carton single cream

Order of cooking

1. Prepare and cook crunchy stuffed courgettes
2. Cook creamy potatoes
3. Prepare strawberries
4. Cook broccoli (over potatoes)

Crunchy Stuffed Courgettes
Serves 2
V Ve

Ingredients
- 2 large courgettes
- 1 tablespoon (15ml) oil
- ½ onion, finely chopped
- 100g mushrooms, finely chopped
- 1 dessertspoon (10ml) tomato purée
- 1 tablespoon (15ml) white wine *or* sherry
- sprinkling of dried tarragon
- salt and pepper
- 25g roasted chopped hazelnuts

Method
Preheat the oven to 190°C/375°F/Gas 5. Cut each courgette in half lengthways. Carefully score a line parallel to the end of the courgette and running down each side. You can then gently spoon out the inside, leaving a boat-like shell. Chop the flesh finely and fry in the oil with the onion and mushrooms for 2–3 minutes. Add the tomato purée, wine or sherry, tarragon and seasoning. Stir well and simmer gently for 2 minutes. Lay the courgette shells in a roasting tin, fill with the cooked mixture and sprinkle with the nuts. Bake in the preheated oven for 25 minutes.

Steamed Broccoli
Serves 2
❋ ☉ **V Ve**

Ingredients
- 200g broccoli florets

Method
Place the broccoli in a steamer or metal colander over a pan of boiling water. Cover and cook for 8 minutes.

Creamy Potatoes
Serves 2
🕘 **V**

Ingredients
    200g new potatoes, unpeeled
    knob of butter
    ½ onion, chopped
    80g Boursin
    4 tablespoons (60ml) milk

Method
Boil the potatoes until ready (approximately 15–20 minutes). Melt the butter and gently fry the onion for 2–3 minutes. Add the Boursin and milk. Stir while this melts down to make a sauce. When the potatoes are ready, drain and mix with sauce before serving.

Strawberries and Cream
Serves 2
✳ 🕘 **V**

Ingredients
    200g punnet of strawberries
    150ml carton single cream

Method
Hull the strawberries and cut each in half (unless they are very small, in which case they can be left whole). Divide between two bowls and serve cream separately.

15 Sweet Things

Everyone likes a treat now and again. Although students do not often bother with desserts, occasionally you will want to indulge yourself. These recipes are very easy to make – in fact I like to think they are foolproof, although I know there are those who somehow will manage to go astray . . . Everyone has a disaster some time. A friend recently reminded me of the occasion when I made a cake which came out flat as a pancake – I had forgotten to put in the flour! And not so long ago we waited rather a long time for a cake to cook, as someone (who shall remain nameless) hadn't turned the oven on!

I fondly remember the pancake parties that one of our friends used to give. He was an absolute ace at pancakes and provided lots of scrummy fillings. As long as we kept him supplied with drinks, he kept us supplied with pancakes. We helped ourselves as the pancakes arrived – and just kept going until we were in danger of bursting!

Banana Hobnob Crunch
Serves 1
✳ ◷ **V**

Ingredients
    1 small banana, mashed
    100g pot banana fromage frais
    2 chocolate Hobnob biscuits, crumbled

Method
Mix together the banana purée and the fromage frais. Layer the banana mixture and the biscuit crumbs into a small bowl, finishing with a layer of crumbs.

Pancakes
Serves 2–3
✳ ◷ **V**

Ingredients
    100g flour
    pinch of salt
    1 egg, beaten
    250ml milk
    oil *or* butter for frying
    sugar (for serving)
    lemon (for serving)

Method
Sift the flour and salt into a bowl. Make a well in the middle and pour the egg and half the milk into it. Beat together well, gradually adding more milk until you have a smoother thin batter. Heat a little oil or butter in a small frying pan and ladle in just enough pancake mixture to cover the bottom of the pan. Cook until the bottom of the pancake starts to brown (lift pancake at the edge to check). Flip(!) the pancake over and cook the other side for a minute or two. Slide on to a serving plate and sprinkle with sugar and a squeeze of lemon.

Baked Apples
Serves 4
V Ve

Ingredients
>   4 large Bramley apples, cored
>   3 tablespoons mincemeat

Method
Preheat the oven to 180°C/350°F/Gas 4. Score around the middle of the apples and put in a baking dish. Fill each apple cavity with the mincemeat. Pour 2 tablespoons (30ml) water into the baking dish and cook in the preheated oven for 45–60 minutes until the apples are soft.

Mum's baked apples
My mother makes baked apples as above but uses a mixture of sultanas, butter and sugar instead of mincemeat to stuff the apples.

Danish Apple Pudding
Serves 4
🕐 **V**

Ingredients
>   1kg Bramley apples, peeled and diced
>   75g butter
>   honey, golden syrup *or* sugar to taste
>   150g fresh wholemeal breadcrumbs
>   50g soft dark brown sugar

Method
Cook the apples with 25g of the butter until very soft (takes about 6–8 minutes). Mash into a purée and sweeten to taste. Leave to cool. Meanwhile, heat the remaining butter and fry the breadcrumbs with the brown sugar until they start to crisp. Leave to cool. When both purée and crumbs are cold, layer into 4 small serving bowls, alternating layers of fruit with crumbs, finishing with a layer of crumbs.

Apple Crumble
Serves 4–8
V

Ingredients
>1kg Bramley apples, peeled and cut into chunks
>2 tablespoons butter
>2 tablespoons caster sugar
>75g self-raising wholemeal flour
>75g soft dark brown sugar
>75g butter, chopped

Method
Preheat the oven to 200°C/400°F/Gas 6. Cook the apples with the 2 tablespoons of butter, until soft but not falling apart. Stir in the caster sugar and put in a pie dish or small casserole dish. Using your fingertips, rub together the flour, brown sugar and chopped butter until the mixture resembles breadcrumbs. Cover the fruit with the crumb mixture and bake in the preheated oven for 30 minutes until the topping begins to brown.

Plum and Raisin Oat-topped Crumble
Serves 1–2
V

If the plums are not ripe enough to stone easily, stew them whole and remove the stones afterwards.

Ingredients
>   200g ripe dessert plums, halved and stoned
>   1 tablespoon (15ml) orange juice
>   1 tablespoon sugar
>   1 tablespoon raisins

For the crumble
>   2 tablespoons plain wholemeal flour
>   25g butter *or* margarine
>   1 tablespoon sugar
>   2 tablespoons porridge oats

Method
Preheat the oven to 200°C/400°F/Gas 6. Gently stew the plums, orange juice, sugar and raisins until soft and syrupy (about 15 minutes.) Put into a small casserole or pie dish. Using your fingertips rub together the flour and butter or margarine until they resemble breadcrumbs, then add the sugar and oats. Cover the plums with the crumble mixture. Cook in the preheated oven for 20–25 minutes until beginning to brown.

Mummy's Baked Custard
Serves 2–3
V

You can improve the texture of your custard by placing the custard dish in a roasting tin with enough boiling water to come halfway up the dish. Then bake as below.

Ingredients
> 2 whole eggs and 1 yolk
> 1 tablespoon sugar
> few drops of vanilla essence
> 250ml milk
> grated nutmeg (optional)
> knob of butter

Method
Preheat the oven to 150°C/300°F/Gas 2. Beat together the eggs, yolk, sugar and vanilla essence. Put the milk into a small saucepan and bring up to boiling point. Remove from the heat immediately, pour on to the egg and sugar mixture and stir well. Strain into a greased pie dish or small casserole dish and sprinkle with grated nutmeg (if using). Put a little knob of butter on top and bake in the preheated oven for 40–60 minutes until the custard has set and a skin has formed.

Rice Pudding
Serves 2–3
V

Ingredients
- 2 tablespoons pudding rice
- 1 tablespoon sugar
- 500ml milk
- knob of butter
- grated nutmeg (optional)

Method
Preheat the oven to 150°C/300°F/Gas 2. Put the rice, sugar and milk in a greased pie dish or small casserole dish. Top with little pieces of butter and sprinkle with grated nutmeg (if using). Bake in the preheated oven for about 2 hours, until the rice has absorbed the milk and a skin has formed.

Greek Honey-nut Pie
Serves 4–6
V

This is an incredibly rich recipe – but utterly delicious! You must serve it in small portions and only on special occasions, as I hate to think what it does to the waistline! Sweet pastry shells can be bought in most large supermarkets and are very good (and I suspect may work out cheaper than making your own).

Ingredients
- 3 tablespoons caster sugar
- 3 tablespoons (45ml) Greek honey
- 3 tablespoons (45ml) double cream
- 75g butter, chopped
- 150g mixed nuts, such as pecans and hazelnuts, chopped
- 190g sweet pastry shell

Method
Preheat the oven to 190°C/375°F/Gas 5. In a small pan dissolve the sugar in the honey, stirring over a gentle heat, then boil for 3 minutes. Add the cream and butter and beat well. Stir in the nuts and pour into the pastry shell. Level the top and bake in the preheated oven for 25–30 minutes.

Banoffee Pie
Serves 6–8
V

It is very important to stir all the time you are heating the toffee mixture. I had a very nasty experience once when I was so busy chatting to someone that I forgot. You will find lots of horrible burnt bits appear if you follow my example – so don't forget to keep stirring!

Ingredients
> 1 sweet pastry shell
> 2 bananas, mashed
> 150g butter
> 2 tablespoons brown sugar
> 400g can sweetened condensed milk
> aerosol can whipping cream

Method
Cover the base of the pastry shell with the mashed banana. Melt the butter gently with the sugar. Do not boil. Add the condensed milk and bring slowly to the boil, stirring all the time. As soon as the mixture begins to bubble, turn the heat right down and simmer gently for a few minutes, stirring throughout until you have a lovely thick toffee-like mixture. Pour over the banana. Chill for at least one hour. Before serving, cover completely with the whipped cream.

Strawberry Cheesecake
Serves 4–6
V

If you are an ethical vegetarian you can obtain jelly crystals in health food shops. If you are not so strict you could use a jelly mix (which contains gelatine).

Ingredients
>   70g butter
>   125g digestives, crushed
>   1 sachet vegetarian strawberry jelly crystals
>   75ml double cream, lightly whipped
>   250g strawberry fromage frais
>   225g punnet of strawberries, halved
>   2–3 tablespoons strawberry jam

Method
Line a 20cm flan tin with foil. Melt the butter in a small pan, add the biscuits and stir well. Press this mixture into the base of the tin and level. Chill. Dissolve the jelly crystals in 125ml boiling water. Then make the jelly up to 200ml with cold water. Leave to cool. When jelly is cool, but not yet beginning to set, mix with the whipped cream and fromage frais and pour on to the biscuit base. Leave to set in the fridge (approximately 1 1/2-2 hours). When filling has set, cover with strawberries. Melt the jam over a gentle heat and spoon over the strawberries. Take out of the tin and remove foil carefully just before serving.

Trifle
Serves 6–8
✳ **V**

Ingredients
8 trifle sponges
2 tablespoons raspberry jam
125ml (5 fl oz) sherry
20 ratafia biscuits, crushed
70g packet instant custard mix
400g can mango slices, drained
1 banana, sliced

For decoration
250ml carton whipping cream
whole ratafia biscuits
fresh raspberries *or* hundreds and thousands and/*or*
silver dragées *or* chopped roasted nuts

Method
Split the trifle sponges and sandwich together with the jam.
Arrange in a serving bowl and spoon in the sherry. Cover
with the crushed ratafia biscuits. Make up the instant custard
according to the instructions on the packet. Cool slightly.
Add the mango and banana to the trifle and cover with
custard. Chill. Whip the cream, spoon over the cold trifle
and arrange your chosen decoration on top.

Brown Bread and Raisin Ice-cream
Serves 4
V

This is utterly delectable, but can be made even naughtier by using Greek yogurt instead of the low-fat yogurt I have used in this version. I don't know if you should risk making this if you live in hall, as it must be left in the freezer compartment of the refrigerator and in a communal kitchen this could be risky. It would be tragic to discover that someone else had been unable to resist your delicious dessert! By the way, don't panic about the state of the baking tray when you have cooked the breadcrumbs, just soak it in water and it will clean easily.

Ingredients
2 large slices wholemeal bread, crumbed
6 tablespoons soft brown sugar
140ml carton whipping cream
300g low-fat natural yogurt
50g raisins

Method
Preheat the oven to 200°C/400°F/Gas 6. Mix together the breadcrumbs and sugar and spread over a baking tray. Bake in the preheated oven for 10 minutes. Whip the cream until it forms soft peaks, then stir in the yogurt and raisins. Mix in the caramelised breadcrumbs and put into a freezer-proof container. Freeze for 4 hours, then transfer to the fridge for 30 minutes before serving.

Peanut Crumblies
Makes 16 biscuits
◷ **V**

Ingredients
>100g butter, softened
>100g crunchy peanut butter
>100g soft brown sugar
>150g plain flour

Method
Preheat the oven to 190°C/375°F/Gas 5. Cream together the butters and sugar until fluffy. Stir in the flour and mix to a dough using 1–2 teaspoons (5–10ml) water to help. Divide into 16, roll into little balls and place these on two non-stick baking trays. Using a dampened fork flatten each ball into a biscuit (but make sure they are not sticking to the trays). Bake in the preheated oven for 15–20 minutes. Leave on the trays for 10 minutes before very carefully transferring to a wire rack to cool.

Oat Crunchies
Makes 16 biscuits
◷ **V**

Ingredients
>100g butter, softened
>50g soft brown sugar
>100g plain flour
>100g porridge oats

Method
Preheat the oven to 190°C/375°F/Gas 5. Cream together the butter and sugar until fluffy. Mix in the flour and oats, and use your hands to knead into a dough adding 1–2 teaspoons (5–10ml) water to help. Divide into 16, roll into little balls and place well apart on two non-stick baking trays. Using a dampened fork, flatten each ball into a biscuit (but make sure they are not sticking to the trays). Bake in the preheated oven for 15–20 minutes, until just starting to colour. Transfer carefully to a wire rack to cool.

Flapjacks
Makes 12
V

Ingredients
> 125g soft margarine
> 125g soft brown sugar
> 1 tablespoon (15ml) golden syrup
> 175g oats

Method
Preheat the oven to 190°C/375°F/Gas 5. Melt the margarine, sugar and syrup together. Stir in the oats. Grease a 28 x 18cm tin and spoon the mixture into it. Press into the base of the tin and level. Bake in the preheated oven for about 20 minutes. Mark into portions but leave in the tin to cool. When cold cut out the individual flapjacks.

Muesli flapjacks
Use the above recipe but add an extra tablespoon (15ml) golden syrup, reduce the amount of oats to 100g and add 100g muesli.

Strawberry Fairy Cakes
Makes 12
V

Ingredients
100g soft margarine or butter
100g caster sugar
100g self-raising flour
2 eggs, beaten

For the buttercream
25g butter, softened
50g icing sugar
few drops of vanilla essence
1–2 teaspoons (5–10ml) milk
12 small strawberries (to decorate)

Method
Preheat the oven to 190°C/375°F/Gas 5. Beat all the cake ingredients together. Spread 12 paper cake cases out on a baking tray and divide the mixture between them. Bake in the preheated oven for about 15 minutes until the cakes are golden brown and feel 'springy' when touched. Leave on a wire rack to cool. Slice off the top of each cake and cut each circle in half making two 'wings'. Make the buttercream by beating the butter, sugar and vanilla essence together, adding just enough milk to form a smooth cream. Put some butter-cream on each cake. Top with a strawberry and then place a 'wing' on each side.

Easy Fruit Cake
Makes 12 portions
V

This is very easy to make and tastes really good. It keeps well in a cake tin and is a great addition to packed lunches.

Ingredients
150g soft margarine
150g muscovado sugar
3 eggs, beaten
200g plain wholemeal flour
1 teaspoon ground cinnamon
500g luxury fruit mix
100g glacé cherries, chopped

Method
Preheat the oven to 170°C/325°F/Gas 3. Beat together the margarine and sugar until creamy. Gently beat in the eggs, a little at a time, adding a little flour with the egg to stop the mixture curdling. Then fold in the remaining flour, cinnamon, fruit mix and cherries. Line a 28 x 18cm baking tin with baking parchment, or greaseproof paper, spoon the mixture into tin and level. Cook in the preheated oven for 55–65 minutes until risen, brown and firm to the touch. Leave in the tin for 5 minutes, then transfer to a wire rack, peel off the baking parchment or greaseproof paper and leave to cool.

Passion Cake
Serves 8–12
V

This recipe comes from *Peckish but Poor*. It has proved incredibly popular – maybe because it scores so highly on the yummy stakes!

Ingredients
>   200g soft margarine
>   200g soft brown sugar
>   4 eggs, beaten
>   200g wholemeal self-raising flour
>   1 teaspoon baking powder
>   300g carrots, peeled and grated
>   grated rind of 1 lemon and 1 tablespoon (15ml) of
>   the juice
>   100g chopped walnuts

For the icing
>   75g cream cheese
>   50g icing sugar
>   grated rind and juice of 1 orange

Method
Preheat the oven to 180°C/350°F/Gas 4. Beat together the margarine, sugar, eggs, flour, baking powder, carrots, lemon rind and juice and walnuts. Put in a greased and lined 20cm deep cake tin. Bake in the preheated oven for about 90 minutes until well risen and golden brown. Leave to cool, while you prepare the icing. Beat together the cream cheese and icing sugar and use just enough orange juice to achieve a creamy consistency. Cover the top of the cake with the icing and sprinkle the orange rind over it.

16 The Slimming Student

This is a tricky topic. With anorexia and bulimia now affecting so many young people, I feel that far too many are trying to lose a few pounds to reach unrealistic weight targets. I definitely belong to the band who would like to see the banning of all fashion advertising and articles which use waif-like models to promote unhealthy images of women. However, as many young people become concerned about their weight at some point, I think it is worth while covering this issue.

The first thing to point out is that if you are maintaining a balanced diet – by this I mean a diet which has a good amount of starchy foods, such as rice, pasta, potatoes and bread, complemented by fresh vegetables and fruit and some proteins, such as beans, nuts and cheese – you will not have many problems with your weight. However, very few people actually stick to this diet. Most of us tend to eat more fats and sugars than we should. And alcohol is very fattening and has no nutritional value.

So if you find yourself putting on a few extra pounds, my advice is to look carefully at your eating habits

before the problem escalates. Are you starting to snack on foodstuffs that are high in either fat or sugar content? If your diet consists of a high proportion of chips, lots of pastry and cheese, crisps and chocolate bars washed down with copious amounts of booze, then you should not be surprised when you start to put on weight! None of these items will hurt if consumed occasionally and in small quantities, but if you want to avoid ballooning you will have to restrict these goodies in your diet. The remedy is obvious: a week or two of a healthy balanced diet, with a ban on the offending goodies and an increase in your exercise regime – you do have an exercise regime don't you? Remember that bodies don't stay young and athletic naturally – should easily do the trick. If you then use a little discretion in the treats you allow yourself each week, you should avoid any further weight problems.

If you are already overweight, following a balanced diet over a few weeks should start to shift those extra pounds (sorry, kilograms!). If this doesn't seem to work, I suggest that a visit to the doctor is in order. Better to be safe than sorry.

I have set out a three-day diet that is easy to follow and will give you an idea of a strict balanced diet. It is not advisable to follow a strict diet for long. You will probably end up bingeing and even heavier than you started. Try this three-day diet and then move on to a normal balanced diet without any treats. This should result in a steady weight loss over a few weeks, then you can slowly start to add some goodies, but only in moderation. I have listed the foods that can be freely eaten on a normal balanced diet and those that should be eaten in moderation or only very occasionally.

3-day diet

Shopping list

6 pieces fruit
450g new potatoes *or* 3 x
    150g baking potatoes
1 lettuce
1 cucumber
1 courgette
2 onions
200g mushrooms
2 tomatoes
1 litre skimmed milk *or*
    500ml semi-skimmed milk
small carton cottage cheese
    and pineapple
small wholemeal loaf

3 choices from breakfast
    variety packs
250ml vegetable soup
200g can BBQ beans
200g can baked beans
225g can pineapple pieces in
    juice
200g can sweetcorn
200g can chopped tomatoes
430g can borlotti beans
oil-free dressing
salt and pepper

Drinks: tea, coffee, water,
    sugar-free drinks

DAY 1

Daily
Milk from allowance
Drinks: tea, coffee, water, sugar-free drinks

Breakfast
variety pack breakfast cereal
milk from allowance

Lunch
vegetable soup
2 slices wholemeal bread
1 piece fruit

Dinner
BBQ beans and pineapple (see page 334)
green salad made with lettuce, ½ cucumber and ½ grated
    courgette, with oil-free dressing
150g boiled new potatoes *or* 150g baked potato (see
    recipe on page 341, but omit margarine)
1 piece fruit

DAY 2

Breakfast
As Day 1

Lunch
small carton cottage cheese and pineapple
2 slices bread
lettuce
1 piece fruit

Dinner
Bean and pineapple salad*
150g boiled new potatoes *or* 150g baked potato
1 piece fruit

DAY 3

Breakfast
As other days

Lunch
2 slices toast
200g can baked beans
1 piece fruit

Dinner
Quick slimmer's stew (see page 335)
150g boiled new potatoes *or* 150g baked potato
1 piece fruit

BBQ Beans and Pineapple
Serves 1
✳ ◔ **V Ve**

Ingredients
> 1 onion, diced
> 100g mushrooms, sliced
> 1 teaspoon (5ml) oil-free dressing
> 200g can BBQ beans
> ½ 225g can pineapple pieces, drained, reserving juice

Method
Stir-fry the onion and mushrooms in the oil-free dressing until soft. Add the BBQ beans, pineapple pieces and 1 tablespoon (15ml) of the reserved juices. Heat through and serve with potato and salad.

Bean and Pineapple Salad
Serves 1
✳ ◔ **V Ve**

Ingredients
> ½ 430g can borlotti beans, drained
> ½ 225g can pineapple pieces, drained, reserving juice
> ½ 200g can sweetcorn
> salt and pepper
> lettuce
> ½ cucumber, sliced
> ½ courgette, grated
> 2 tomatoes, sliced

Method
Mix together the beans, pineapple and sweetcorn. Add 1 tablespoon (15ml) of the reserved juices from the pineapple and season well. Arrange the salad ingredients on a plate and top with the bean mixture.

Quick Slimmer's Stew
Serves 1
V Ve

Ingredients
    1 onion, diced
    200g can chopped tomatoes
    200g can condensed vegetable soup
    100g button mushrooms
    ½ 430g can borlotti beans
    ½ 200g can sweetcorn
    salt and pepper

Method
Preheat the oven to 180°C/350°F/Gas 4. In a small pan, bring the onion, tomatoes and soup to the boil, then simmer for 5 minutes. Add the mushrooms and continue cooking for a further 5 minutes. Transfer to a small casserole dish, add the beans and sweetcorn, season and cook in the preheated oven for 30 minutes.

A balanced diet

A balanced diet should consist of roughly 30 per cent starchy food, 30 per cent fruit and vegetables, 15 per cent lean protein, 15 per cent dairy products and 10 per cent fats.

Foods that can be eaten freely

Fruit and vegetables
Most fruit and vegetables are low in fat and sugar content. (One exception is the avocado which is high in fat.) Therefore they should play a major part in your diet, preferably fresh, but even frozen or canned. However, remember to buy canned fruit in natural juice, not syrup. Do not add sugar to fruit or fat to vegetables when cooking.

Starchy foods
Examples of starchy foods are cereal, rice, pasta, potatoes. These are another very important group of foods as they add bulk to your meals and ensure that you aren't still hungry at the end of a meal. However, it is very important not to add fat because starchy foods can absorb a lot of it and then become a dieter's enemy.

Foods to be eaten in moderation

Lean proteins
These include beans, pulses and lentils. Although nuts are a good source of protein they are very high in natural oils, so always use sparingly.

Dairy products
This group includes butter, milk, cheese and yogurt. As these can all be high in fat, you can either use them more sparingly or swap to the lower-fat varieties such as skimmed milk, low-fat cheeses, spreads and yogurts.

Foods to be eaten only occasionally

Fats
Although we do need some fats in our diet, these are usually provided by the fat content of the other foods we eat. Therefore we need to be very sparing in adding any extra. As well as cutting down the amount of fat we cook with or the dairy products in our diet, we must beware of such high fat foods as ice-cream, salad dressings, cakes, biscuits and pastries, chips and crisps, chocolate and many convenience foods.

Example of a day's balanced diet

Breakfast
wholemeal, sugar-free *or* low-sugar cereal with skimmed milk and fresh fruit

Lunch
baked jacket potato with beans and side salad *or*
vegetable soup with wholemeal roll *or*
sandwich made with wholemeal bread with a spicy bean filling *or* low-fat cheese, with a side salad *or* plenty of salad in the sandwich
piece of fruit

Dinner
Not-so-fattening pasta (see page 338) *or*
rice *or* potato served with vegetables in sauce. For extra protein you could add some beans *or* a small amount of nuts to the sauce or serve with grated cheese
a small portion of fruit and natural yogurt

Not-so-fattening Pasta
Serves 1
⏲ **V Ve**

Contrary to popular belief, you do not have to add fat when you cook and it's not pasta itself that's fattening but what you put on it.

Ingredients
> 200g can chopped tomatoes
> 1 clove garlic, crushed
> 2 teaspoons (10ml) tomato purée
> 75g broccoli florets
> 1 carrot, diced
> 50–75g pasta
> salt and pepper

Method
Put water on to boil for the pasta. In a small pan bring the tomatoes, garlic and tomato purée to the boil, then simmer gently for 15 minutes. Over this pan place a steamer or metal colander and steam the broccoli and carrot. Meanwhile, cook the pasta. Drain, place in a bowl, arrange the broccoli and carrots on top and cover with the tomato sauce. Season well.

17 Lifesavers

As term draws to a close, so often does the bank balance! This is the time when you may have to simplify your diet in order to eke out the remaining pennies until the day when you can head for the comforts of home. This is when the staples of student cooking really come into their own. Pasta, rice, potatoes and bread are all cheap and filling. This is the time to start experimenting with them. Search out the forgotten items at the back of your store cupboard – any dried beans, lentils, or cans will come in very useful. With a few extras such as onions, beans and cheese, you will be amazed at what you can produce.

Bean Soup
Serves 1–2
V

Ingredients
100g dried bean mix, soaked overnight
1 potato (200g), diced
400ml vegetable stock
1 tablespoon (15ml) oil
2 onions, 1 chopped, 1 thinly sliced
2 cloves garlic, crushed
knob of butter
1 teaspoon brown sugar

Method
Boil the bean mix for 10 minutes, then simmer for about 1 hour until the beans are cooked. Cook the potato in the stock for 10 minutes. Heat the oil and fry the chopped onion and garlic for 5 minutes. Mix the cooked beans and fried onion and garlic with the potato and stock. Squash some of the beans and potato against the side of the pan to thicken the soup. Simmer for 10 minutes. Meanwhile, melt the butter and fry the sliced onion with the sugar until brown. When the soup is ready, sprinkle the browned onion on top and serve.

Baked Potatoes
Serves 1
V

Ingredients
> 1–2 potatoes, cleaned
> knob of margarine
> salt and pepper

Method
Preheat the oven to 220°C/425°F/Gas 7. Prick the potatoes all over. Bake in the preheated oven for 1–1½ hours (depending on size). Cut in half and fork in the margarine. Season well. (Extra cash could buy cheese or baked beans to add as a filling.)

Cheese and Marmite jackets
When the potatoes are cooked, scoop out the flesh, mix with margarine, 1 teaspoon (5ml) Marmite and 25g grated cheese. Preheat the grill. Put the skins on an ovenproof tray, fill with the potato mixture and grill until brown.

Spaghetti
Serve 1
❋ ⏱ **V**

Ingredients
> 100g wholemeal spaghetti
> knob of margarine
> salt and black pepper
> sprinkling of oregano

Method
Cook the spaghetti, drain and add the margarine. Season, sprinkle with oregano and serve. (If finances allow, top with some grated cheese.)

Pasta with Tomato and Garlic
Serves 1
✳ ◔ **V**

This is one of those dishes that I often resort to when my husband Andy is away on one of his trips – travelling the world, visiting all those places I'd love to go to, staying in wonderful hotels, eating and drinking his only relaxation after a hard day's work (oh, not forgetting those business lunches). Well, all I can say is it's a hard life for some! This is an ideal recipe for one as it's extremely quick and simple to make.

Ingredients
> 100g pasta
> knob of margarine *or* butter
> 1 tablespoon (15ml) tomato purée
> 1 clove garlic, crushed

Method
Cook the pasta in boiling water, then drain. Return to the pan, add the other ingredients and heat through.

Pasta with Cheese 'n' Herb Sauce
Serves 1
◔ **V**

Ingredients
> 75g pasta
> 1 tablespoon (15ml) oil
> 1 onion, diced
> 3 tablespoons (45ml) milk
> 75g soft cheese, herb and garlic flavoured
> salt and pepper

Method
Cook the pasta in boiling water. Meanwhile, heat the oil and fry the onion until soft and starting to brown at the edges. Add the milk and cheese and stir, until it melts and makes a sauce. Drain the cooked pasta and mix with the sauce. Season and serve.

Oniony Rice
Serves 1
⊕ **V Ve**

This is a cheap, simple recipe that is nevertheless very tasty. I love it with tomato sauce.

Ingredients
>   2 tablespoons (30ml) oil
>   2 onions, 1 chopped, 1 thinly sliced
>   100g rice
>   375ml vegetable stock
>   juice of 1 lemon
>   salt and pepper

Method
Heat 1 tablespoon (15ml) of the oil and fry the chopped onion for 5 minutes until soft. Add the rice and stir through. Put in a saucepan with the stock and bring to the boil, then cover and simmer until the rice is cooked. Meanwhile, fry the sliced onion in the remaining oil until very brown. When the rice is cooked, drain and add lemon juice to taste, season well and serve sprinkled with the browned onion on top.

Rice, Potatoes and Onions
Serves 1
🕐 **V Ve**

Although this is a recipe for when you are utterly broke, don't wait until then to try it. It's really very good. When you're in the money add some mango or lime chutney.

Ingredients
>200g (8 oz) potatoes, diced
>oil for frying
>100g (4 oz) rice
>1 onion, sliced
>1 teaspoon (5ml) sugar
>soy sauce

Method
Fry the potatoes in the oil while cooking the rice. When the potatoes start to colour, add the onion and continue frying until both are browned. Add the sugar and a dash of soy sauce. (This will make the vegetables slightly sticky as the sugar caramelises.) When the rice is ready, arrange on a plate and pour the caramelised vegetables over it.

18 Round-the-World Veggie Dishes

In this chapter I have tried to keep close to authentic recipes. This may entail purchasing some items that you wouldn't normally buy and you will have to decide if you think it is worthwhile or whether you could substitute something else. All these recipes are goodies that we have picked up on our travels. There are no difficult ones – but there are some very tasty ones! Our particular favourites, which are often cooked in our house, are those for cheese fondue (I'm a fondue fanatic), French onion soup, patatas bravas and pilau rice. However, each one is guaranteed to make an appearance at some time during the year. I hope you have fun trying them out – and that you get to eat some of the recipes in the countries they come from.

Tzatziki
Serves 3–4
✳ ⊕ **V**

Ingredients
>   200g Greek yogurt
>   ¼ cucumber, finely chopped
>   1 clove garlic, crushed
>   2 teaspoons (10ml) white wine vinegar
>   1 tablespoon fresh mint, chopped

Method
Mix together all the ingredients and serve as a dip or as a sauce for rice dishes.

Simple Hummus
Serves 2
✳ ⊕ **V**

This is much better than a shop-bought version. You can make it even creamier by substituting Greek yogurt for the natural yogurt. Play around with the amount of garlic and lemon juice that you use to tailor it to your own taste.

Ingredients
>   420g can chick peas, drained
>   1–2 cloves garlic, crushed
>   juice of ½–1 lemon
>   2 tablespoons (30ml) natural yogurt
>   1 tablespoon (15ml) oil

Method
Mash the chick peas until smooth. Add the rest of the ingredients and mix well. Serve with toast or pitta bread.

Hummus
Serves 2–4
* ☉ **V Ve**

Tahini is not absolutely essential to this dish but it does add to its authenticity.

Ingredients
>   400g can chick peas, drained, reserving the liquid
>   juice of 1 lemon
>   2 tablespoons (30ml) tahini (optional)
>   2 cloves garlic, crushed
>   1 tablespoon (15ml) oil

Method
Mash the chick peas to a purée. Gradually add the lemon juice, tahini (if using), garlic, oil and 2 tablespoons (30ml) of the liquid from the can of chick peas, until you have a thick dip. Chill before serving with toast or pitta bread.

French Onion Soup
Serves 2
V

This makes a great meal for two, served with garlic bread and red wine. *Magnifique!*

Ingredients
>   75g butter
>   4 onions, sliced thinly
>   1 tablespoon plain flour
>   1 clove garlic, crushed
>   2 onion stock cubes
>   salt and pepper
>   4 slices French bread
>   50g cheese, grated

Method
Melt the butter and fry the onions for 10 minutes until soft and browning. Stir in the flour and garlic, mixing well. Dissolve the stock cubes in 750ml boiling water, add to the onion mixture and season. Bring to the boil, then simmer for 20 minutes. Preheat the grill. Put the bread on the grill tray, sprinkle with the cheese and grill until it starts to melt. Ladle the soup into bowls and float two slices of bread in each one.

Vichyssoise (Potato and Leek Soup)
Serves 1–2
✳ ☉ **V**

This is a useful recipe for a dinner party. If you have access to a blender/liquidiser, you can make it really special by adding a small tub of crème fraîche and liquidising. You will then have a smooth soup which can also be served cold – with an ice cube or two in the middle and garnished with chopped chives.

Ingredients
> 200g potatoes, diced
> 200g leeks, well washed and chopped
> 375ml vegetable stock
> 125ml milk
> salt and pepper

Method
Put all the ingredients in a saucepan and bring to the boil. Cover and simmer for 20 minutes until the vegetables are soft. Check the seasoning and serve.

Greek Salad
Serves 2
✳ ☉ **V**

Ingredients
> few crunchy salad leaves
> 2 large tomatoes, sliced
> ½ cucumber, diced
> few slices onion
> 2 tablespoons black olives
> 100g feta cheese, diced

For the dressing
> 2 tablespoons (30ml) olive oil
> 2 teaspoons (10ml) wine vinegar
> 1 clove garlic, crushed
> salt and pepper
> squeeze of lemon

Method
Put all the salad ingredients into a bowl. Mix the dressing ingredients and pour over the salad just before serving.

Tabbouleh
Serves 3–4
✳ ◔ **V Ve**

Ingredients
> 100g bulgar wheat
> juice from 1 large *or* 2 small lemons
> salt and pepper
> 4 tablespoons (60ml) olive oil
> 2 tablespoons parsley, finely chopped
> 2 tablespoons mint, finely chopped
> 6 spring onions, sliced
> 2 tomatoes, peeled and diced

Method
Soak the bulgar wheat in boiling water for 10 minutes. Rinse and drain, squeezing out as much water as possible. Put in a bowl, add the lemon juice and season well. Leave to stand for 20 minutes. Now add the remaining ingredients and stir well.

French Dressing
Serves 2–3
✳ ◔ **V Ve**

Ingredients
> 3 tablespoons (45ml) olive oil
> 1 tablespoon (15ml) tarragon *or* white wine vinegar
> 1 teaspoon mustard powder
> 1 teaspoon caster sugar
> 1 teaspoon salt
> sprinkling of black pepper
> 1 clove garlic, crushed (optional)

Method
Whisk or shake all the ingredients together.

Imam Bayildi (The Priest Fainted)
Serves 4–6
V Ve

A dish that we discovered in Turkey and that I frequently make during the summer months. Serve with lots of crusty French bread to mop up the juices.

Ingredients
- 1 onion, chopped
- 2 cloves garlic, crushed
- olive oil
- 1 aubergine, cut into slices lengthways
- 400g can chopped tomatoes
- 2 tablespoons (30ml) tomato purée
- 2 tablespoons fresh parsley, chopped

Method
Preheat the oven to 180°C/350°F/Gas 4. Heat some oil and fry the onion and garlic until soft. Put in a casserole dish. Fry the aubergine slices, a few at a time, transferring to the casserole as they brown. (You will need a lot of oil for this.) Then add the remaining ingredients and bake in the pre-heated oven for 45 minutes. Drizzle with more oil before serving. Serve cold.

Patatas Bravas
Serves 2
🕐 **V**

If there is one dish that I absolutely could not live without, this is it. I like potato dishes and this one has a heavenly sauce. We are very keen tapas fans, although it's got to be said that there are some pretty ropy imitations of tapas bars around. But there are also some real gems. Our favourite is in Brighton, Casa Don Carlos (run by Carlos, of course). His patatas bravas are great, as is everything on the menu. This is my version.

Ingredients
300g new potatoes, unpeeled
oil for shallow frying

For the sauce
2 tablespoons (30ml) olive oil
1 tablespoon (15ml) tomato purée
2 teaspoons (10ml) wine vinegar
1 teaspoon paprika
1 tablespoon (15ml) single cream (optional)

Method
Boil the potatoes for 10–15 minutes until just tender but not soft. Drain and cool, cut into halves or quarters depending on size. Heat the oil and fry the potatoes until brown. Mix the sauce ingredients together and pour over potatoes. Serve.

Gratin Dauphinois
Serves 4
V

Ingredients
>   knob of butter *or* margarine
>   2 cloves garlic, crushed
>   1kg potatoes, sliced very thinly
>   75g cheese, grated
>   salt and pepper
>   125ml carton double cream
>   125ml milk

Method
Preheat the oven to 180°C/350°F/Gas 4. Grease a shallow casserole or lasagne dish with the butter or margarine and spread one of the garlic cloves over the bottom. Arrange a layer of potatoes in the dish and sprinkle with one third of the cheese. Season. Repeat the procedure twice. Finally mix together the cream, milk and remaining clove of garlic and pour over the potatoes. Bake in the preheated oven for 1 hour or until browned on top.

Refried Beans
Serves 2
✳ ⊙ **V Ve**

Ingredients
>   400g can pinto beans, drained
>   3 tablespoons (45ml) groundnut oil
>   1 onion, chopped
>   1 clove garlic, crushed
>   salt and pepper
>   sprinkling chilli powder *or* sauce

Method
Mash the beans roughly. Heat the oil and fry the onion and garlic until soft and golden. Add the beans and stir-fry for 2–3 minutes. Season to taste. Use as an accompaniment for Mexican dishes or to fill burritos or tacos.

Pilau Rice

Serves 2–4

✳ ◕ **V**

We often eat curries in our house, so I keep a number of whole spices in my store cupboard. If you too are a curry fanatic, then I think that it is worthwhile investing in a few spices – they really add an authentic touch to your cooking. This recipe for pilau rice is very popular and better than many of the versions you find in Indian takeaways.

Ingredients

150g basmati rice, soaked
1 tablespoon (15ml) oil
½ teaspoon whole coriander seeds
½ teaspoon whole cumin seeds
½ teaspoon whole cardamom seeds
1 teaspoon turmeric
375ml vegetable stock
knob of butter

Method

I like to leave the rice to soak in cold water for 10–15 minutes before using. If this isn't possible, at least put it in a sieve and run plenty of cold water through it. Heat the oil and fry the spices for about one minute, stirring well. Then add the rice, give a good stir and pour in the stock. Stir again, cover with a tight-fitting lid and bring to the boil. Simmer gently for 10–12 minutes until all the stock has been absorbed. Take off the heat, add the butter, cover and leave to stand for 10 minutes before serving.

Spanish Tortilla
Serves 2–3
✳ ⊕ **V**

Do pay attention to the fact that for this dish you must have a frying pan that can go under the grill. That is, not only must it fit under the grill but it must have a *heat-proof* handle. If you are the proud possessor of a frying pan with a plastic handle and you try this recipe you will end up with a rather deformed handle! (The time I saw someone fall into this trap it was not even their pan – I don't think the owner ever worked out what had happened.)

Ingredients
>   3 tablespoons (45ml) oil
>   300g potato, finely cubed
>   knob of butter
>   1 onion, diced
>   2 cloves garlic, crushed
>   1 red pepper, diced
>   4 eggs, beaten
>   pinch of oregano
>   salt and pepper

Method
Heat the oil and fry the potato until cooked and browned (about 6–8 minutes). Remove the potato from the pan, add the butter and fry the onion, garlic and pepper for 5 minutes. Return the potato to the pan and pour in the eggs which will quickly begin to set. Sprinkle with oregano and season. Cook on a low heat for 2 minutes. Preheat the grill. Put the frying pan under the grill and cook until the top of the tortilla is golden brown. Slide on to a plate and cut into wedges. Serve with crusty bread and salad – or unauthentically with baked beans and grilled tomatoes.

Calzone
Serves 2
V

If you have never tried these before you are in for a treat. They are a little different from the version my friend Stuart first introduced me to, which merely involved taking one shop-bought pizza, cooking it and then folding it in half and eating it as a sandwich. You could try his way but I think that you will find my way quite a lot tastier. I sometimes substitute a soft garlic and herb flavoured cheese for the ricotta.

Ingredients
>2 tablespoons (30ml) oil
>1 onion, diced
>1 clove garlic, crushed
>1 red pepper, finely diced
>100g mushrooms, chopped
>1 packet pizza dough mix
>2 tablespoons (30ml) tomato purée
>sprinkling of oregano
>125g ricotta cheese
>50g cheese, grated
>salt and pepper

Method
Preheat the oven to 200°C/400°F/Gas 6. Heat the oil and fry the onion, garlic, pepper and mushrooms until browning. Make up the pizza dough as directed on the packet. Divide into two and flatten each into a 16cm round. Spread them with the tomato purée and sprinkle with oregano. Mix the cooked vegetables with the cheeses and divide between the rounds. Season well. Fold each round in half and pinch down the edges, so that you have two pizza pasties. Put on a baking tray and cook in the preheated oven for 20–30 minutes until well risen and brown.

Cheese Boreks
Serves 4
🕐 **V**

Some cookery writers make a big fuss about using filo pastry but I find it very easy to use and don't bother with damp tea towels, etc. Just don't go walkabout in the middle of making these because the pastry will become crisp and unusable if left too long.

Ingredients
    100g feta cheese, crumbled
    1 egg, beaten
    1 tablespoon fresh chopped mint
    4 sheets filo pastry
    25g melted butter

Method
Preheat the oven to 180°C/350°F/Gas 4. Mix together the cheese, egg and mint. Cut each sheet of filo pastry into 3 equal lengths and brush with the melted butter. Place a large teaspoon of mixture at one end of each strip of pastry, roll pastry over filling twice, then fold ends in and continue rolling, so that you have a neat cigar shape with the filling completely enclosed. Put on a greased baking tray and brush with butter. Repeat until you have 12 boreks. Bake in the preheated oven for about 15 minutes until crisp and golden.

Burritos (Stuffed Tortillas)
Serves 2
🕐 **V**

Ingredients
    4 flour tortillas
    Refried Beans (page 352)
    2 tablespoons (30ml) canned chopped tomatoes
    50g cheese, grated

Method
Preheat the oven to 180°C/350°F/Gas 4. Lay out the tortillas and place a tablespoon of refried beans in the middle of each one. Top with the tomatoes and cheese. Fold each tortilla into a parcel, place in an ovenproof dish and cook in the preheated oven for 20 minutes. Serve with salsa, sour cream and guacamole (recipes on page 290).

Pistou
Serves 2–4
✳ **V**

Ingredients
> 2 tablespoons (30ml) olive oil
> 1 onion, chopped
> 1 clove garlic, crushed
> 200g carrots, diced
> 1 green *or* red pepper, diced
> 400g can chopped tomatoes
> 250ml vegetable stock
> 50g small pasta shapes
> 1–2 tablespoons (15–30ml) pesto

Method
Heat the oil and cook the onion, garlic, carrots and pepper until soft. Add the tomatoes and stock and bring to the boil. Cover and simmer for 15 minutes. Add the pasta shapes and cook for a further 10 minutes. Stir in the pesto and serve with crusty French bread.

Cheese Fondue
Serves 4
✳ ◐ **V**

This is still popular in our house – though not so much with Andy. Unfortunately he broke the fondue pot I had bought in Switzerland and I'm insisting that I need another trip there to replace it!

Ingredients
> 300ml dry white wine
> 400g Cheddar, grated
> 200g Gruyère *or* Emmental, grated
> 4 teaspoons cornflour
> miniature of vodka *or* gin
> large fresh baguette, cut into big chunks

Method
Heat the wine in a large saucepan. Add the cheeses. Cook for a few minutes, stirring constantly, until the cheeses melt. Dissolve the cornflour in the vodka or gin and add to the mixture, continuing to stir until the fondue thickens. Serve in bowls with chunks of crusty bread to dip.

Spiced Couscous
Serves 4
🕐 **V**

This is quite a spicy dish; the cinnamon gives it a very unusual taste.

Ingredients
    1 aubergine (200g), cubed
    1 potato (200g), cut into matchsticks
    200g carrots, sliced
    375ml vegetable stock
    2 tablespoons (30ml) oil
    1 onion, sliced
    1 pepper, diced
    4 cloves garlic, crushed
    1 teaspoon chilli powder
    1 teaspoon cinnamon
    1 teaspoon ground ginger
    400g can chopped tomatoes
    200g couscous
    50g butter
    100g raisins
    50g toasted almonds

Method
Put the aubergine, potato, carrots and stock in a saucepan, bring to the boil, then cover and simmer for 20 minutes until the vegetables are tender. Meanwhile, heat the oil and fry the onion, pepper and garlic until soft. Add the spices, stir-fry for 1 minute, pour in the tomatoes and simmer for 10 minutes. Cook the couscous as directed on the packet and mix with the butter, raisins and almonds. Strain the boiled vegetables and add to the tomato mixture. Serve the couscous with the vegetables over the top.

Veggie Bobotie
Serves 4
V

Since the changes in South Africa, Andy has found himself a frequent visitor to that beautiful country. He has even been lucky enough to be invited to stay in a private house instead of always having to stay in hotels. The cuisine is something that he has been very impressed with. This is my version of one of their national dishes.

Ingredients
>   1 tablespoon (15ml) oil
>   1 onion, chopped
>   1 clove garlic, crushed
>   1 tablespoon (15ml) medium curry paste
>   400g Vegemince
>   1 large slice wholemeal bread, soaked in 3
>   tablespoons (45ml) water
>   8 ready to eat apricots, chopped
>   2 large bananas
>   salt and pepper
>   2 eggs, beaten
>   250ml milk
>   pinch of turmeric

Method
Preheat the oven to 180°C/350°F/Gas 4. Heat the oil and fry the onion and garlic until soft, add the curry paste and cook for 2 minutes. Add the Vegemince and 375ml water and simmer for 5 minutes. Mash the bread and stir in, together with the apricots. Mash one banana and add to the mixture. Season. Transfer to an ovenproof dish. Cover and bake in the preheated oven for 20 minutes. Beat the eggs, milk and turmeric together. Remove the dish from the oven, uncover and pour in the egg mixture. Slice the remaining banana lengthways and arrange over the top. Bake, uncovered, for another 30 minutes until the top is firm and golden. Serve hot.

Leftovers

Capers
Spaghetti Putanesca (page 50)
Capers go well with any tomato-based sauces.

Celery
Caponata (page 98)
Jambalaya (page 114)
Use chopped celery in salads or mixed with cheese as a sandwich filling.

Crème fraîche
Eggs Florentine (page 148)
Mushroom Stroganoff (page 13)
Tricolor Spaghetti (page 48)

Eggs
Chinese Omelette Rolls (page 15)
Egg and Lentil Curry (page 39)
Huevos Rancheros (page 198)
Kidney Bean Kedgeree (page 20)
Omelette (page 144)
Pipérade (page 36)
Scrambled Curried Eggs with Chapattis (page 31)
Toasted Omelette Sandwich (page 35)
Tomato and Herb Omelette (page 22)

2 eggs
Huevos Rancheros (page 198)
Kidney Bean Kedgeree (page 20)
Omelette (page 144)
Pipérade (page 36)
Toasted Omelette Sandwich (page 35)

3 eggs
Egg and Lentil Curry (page 39)
Scrambled Curried Eggs with Chapattis (page 31)
Tomato and Herb Omelette (page 22)

½ green pepper
Chicken and Banana Creole (page 42)
Coconut Chicken Curry (page 120)
Green Curry (page 78)

Herbs
Baked Tomatoes in Cheesy Cream (page 168)
Roasted New Potatoes (page 170)

Mascarpone
Mascarpone Macaroni Cheese (page 155)
Mascarpone and Tomato Sauce for pasta (page 150)

Mozzarella
Aubergines Baked with Cheese (page 154)
Chilli Pizza (page 24)
Italian Fish Bake (page 86)
Pizza Margherita (page 24)

½ red pepper
Bean Salsa (page 11)
Quick Curry for One (page 84)
Red Pepper and Mushroom Kebabs (page 18)
Toasted Omelette Sandwich (page 35)

Salsa
Avocado and Salsa Tortillas (page 29)

Savoy Cabbage
Japaneasy Noodles (page 174)
Pot-roasted Chicken (page 128)
Stir-fried Greens (page 165)
West Country Chicken (page 121)

Soft cheese
Dolcelatte-dressed Spaghetti and Leeks (page 16)
Tuna-stuffed Jacket Potatoes (page 19)
Soft cheese mixed with grated or chopped celery or chopped
spring onions makes a good filling for sandwiches or rolls.

Soft cheese with garlic
Broccoli Sauce (page 142)
Chick Peas and Veg (page 143)
Creamed Leek and Courgette Sauce (page 142)
Garlicky Beans (page 28)

Sour cream
Avocado and Salsa Tortillas (page 29)
Kidney Bean Kedgeree (page 20)

Spring onions
Avocado and Salsa Tortillas (page 29)
Bean Salsa (page 11)
Chicken Chow Mein (page 23)
Hot 'n' Spicy Noodles (page 175)
Spaghetti Tunagnese (page 146)
Thai Lamb (page 41)

Sun-dried tomatoes
Tricolor Spaghetti (page 48)
Vegetarian Pasta Bake (page 131)

Thai red curry paste
Chinese Prawns (page 26)
Spaghethai Bolognese (page 71)
Thai Crispy Vegetables (page 40)
Thai Peanutty Pork (page 87)
Thai Prawn Curry (page 89)

Index

Brie and grape sandwich 190
broccoli, cheese and tomato quiche 231
cheese dip 288
cheese 'n' herb sauce with pasta 342
cheese 'n' lentil bake 241
cheese and nut risotto 69
cheese and potato cakes 210
cheese and tomato vegetables 210
croque monsieur 30
Dolcelatte-dressed spaghetti and leeks 16
feta-filled filo 74
fondue 246, 357
gratins 85, 159, 352
Greek feta and vegetable casserole 76
grilled cheesy mash 251
jacket potatoes with garlic cheese and mushrooms 14
macaroni cheese 155
and mango toasties 193
and Marmite jacket potatoes 341
mascarpone and tomato sauce 150
and mushroom cannelloni 238
omelettes 144, 223
quick fried pizzas 211
ricotta with honey and pine nuts 306
in salads 105, 205
sauce 270
spicy cheese and nut pâté 194
toasted cheese 192

veggies in cheese sauce 216
chick peas
with banana and mango 235
cauliflower cheese and bean gratin 159
cauliflower, chick pea and tomato curry 57
chick pea curry 219
and chicken stew 112
curried bean and fruit salad 227
hummus 346–7
stuffed pitta breads 55
and veg 143
chicken
baked lemon chicken 32
and banana creole 42
and chick pea stew 112
chicken noodles 43
chow mein 23
coconut chicken curry 120
coronation chicken salad 135
garlic chicken 132
jambalaya 114
lemon chicken with olives 116
lime-fried chicken 125
and mango pilau 83
pot-roasted chicken 128
roasted coconut chicken 122
roasted with vegetables 134
Sri Lankan curry 88
sticky fingers chicken 111
tandoori chicken 77
teriyaki stir-fry 91
West Country chicken 121
x-tra nice chicken 127
chocolate tiramisu 291

cinnamon rock buns 185
courgettes
    and carrot stir-fry 215
    divine summer soup 196
    and leek sauce 142
    ratatouille 158, 236–7
    stir-fried courgettes 166
    stuffed courgettes 311
    tomato, cheese and
        courgette salad 205
    and walnuts 17
couscous
    curry-style couscous 177
    with fruit and nuts 106
    spiced couscous 358
curries
    aubergine dupiaza 261
    aubergine, mushroom and
        coriander balti 235
    bean dhansak 295
    bhindi bhajee 296
    cauliflower, chick pea and
        tomato curry 57
    chick pea curry 219
    coconut chicken curry 120
    dhal and spinach curry 79
    egg and lentil curry 39
    fruity curry sauce 220
    golden bean curry 27
    green curry 78
    lamb korma 54
    potato and tomato curry
        156
    quick creamy curry sauce 8
    quick curry for one 84
    sabzi curry 119
    scrambled curried eggs 31
    Sri Lankan curry 88
    tandoori chicken 77
    ten-minute curry 218
    Thai prawn curry 89
    tikka masala sauce 145
    undercover beans 25

vegetable and nut curry
    268
custard, baked 318

eggs
    boiled eggs 199
    carrot, egg and olive salad
        104
    Chinese omelette rolls 15
    Chinese rice with omelette
        221
    egg fried rice 300
    egg and lentil curry 39
    egg, tomato and mushroom
        fry-up 198
    egg and vegetable hash
        197
    eggs florentine 148
    huevos rancheros 198
    Niçoise salad 113
    omelettes 22, 144, 223
    pipérade 36
    scrambled curried eggs 31
    scrambled eggs 195
    Spanish tortilla 354
    toasted omelette sandwich
        35

fajitas 289
fish
    Italian fish bake 86
    see also anchovies; tuna
flapjacks 186, 325
fondue 246, 357
French onion soup 347
fruit cake 327

gado gado salad 49
garlic bread 267
garlic dip 287
goulash 272
guacamole 290